THE

TOUR

OF

Doctor Syntax,

IN

SEARCH OF THE PICTURESQUE,

A Poem.

BY

WILLIAM COMBE.

WITH AN INTERESTING BIOGRAPHY OF THE AUTHOR.

Ut Pictura, Poësis erit, quæ, si propius stes,
Te capiat magis, et quædam, si longius abstes;
Hæc amat obscurum, volet hæc sub luce videri,
Judicis argutum quæ non formidat acumen:
Hæc placuit semel, hæc decies repetita placebit.

HORAT. *Ars Poetica.*

ILLUSTRATED BY

T. ROWLANDSON

NEW YORK:
JAMES MILLER, 647 BROADWAY.
1872.

PREFACE;

WITH

A LIFE OF THE AUTHOR.

THE origin of DR. SYNTAX is well known to the mature portion of the reading public; but as his acquaintance will, doubtless, be eagerly sought by many of more recent standing, it may not be out of place here, to recapitulate the circumstances attendant on his literary birth.

The late Mr. ACKERMANN was the publisher of a monthly periodical, called The Poetical Magazine, to which the celebrated caricaturist, ROWLANDSON, was engaged to furnish occasional embellishments. It was determined, by way of giving them additional interest, to produce a series of consecutive illustrations of some one subject.

The idea of a Tour, by an eccentric Clergyman and Schoolmaster, enthusiastically in love with letters and the arts, was decided on, and the plates were executed in monthly succession.

Mr. Combe was, at that period, engaged as a contributor to the Magazine, and, as each plate was finished, he adapted a narration in verse to it, which was published, with the plate, in the next month's number. The artist and the poet worked independently of each other, without any preconcerted plan, and in entire ignorance of each other's progress or intentions. The whole was afterwards published as a volume, and thus was produced a work which excited more attention, and has enjoyed a greater degree of public favour than was ever bestowed on any other publication of its class.

The life of the talented author of Doctor Syntax was not more singular for the dissipation which marked the commencement of his career, than for the extraordinary application which characterized his maturer years, and the lateness of the period at which he attained the zenith of his popularity; and it is presumed that a few particulars of his history will be acceptable.

William Combe was born of parents in good circumstances, who placed him at Eton school, and in due time afterwards sent him to Oxford. His uncle, a Mr. Alexander, an Alderman of London, left him sixteen thousand pounds, on the receipt of which he determined to study the law. With this view he left the university, entered himself of the Temple, and was called to the bar. His handsome person, however, and mental accomplishments soon led him into circles of society and a course of expenditure far beyond his means, and ultimately involved him in the very depths of distress. In his days of prosperity, the splendour of his dress and ménage in general, together with his highly aristocratic deportment, had gained him the appellation of Duke Combe.

His emergencies at length drove him to enlist as a soldier, and at Wolverhampton he was recognised by an old acquaintance, crawling through the streets, after a long march, dusty and lame, in quest of his quarters. His friend exclaimed, "Is it possible that I behold you, Combe, and bearing a knapsack?" "Pooh!" said the fallen hero, "a philosopher ought to bear anything." At the public-house at which he was billeted, his literary acquirements excited such astonishment that the house was nightly filled with customers who came to wonder at the soldier who knew Greek. Roger Kemble was then at the same town, with his strolling company, and gave him a benefit, which furnished the means of obtaining his discharge. On this occasion he spoke an address, in which it was intimated that he would solve the mystery of his extraordinary situation. After noticing the various rumours respecting him, he concluded it thus:—"Now, ladies and gentlemen, I am going to tell you what I am—I am, ladies and gentlemen—your most humble and grateful servant." So saying, he disappeared. Soon after this, an old college acquaintance found him officiating as under-waiter at a tavern in a Welsh watering-place. He subsequently entered into the French army; and, at another period, his exigencies imparted such charms to the soup-pots of a French monastery, that he was about to assume the cowl. While the monks were effecting his conversion, and during the requisite probation, however, he grew in good case, and other prospects opening to him, he went to London again. There he obtained employment among the booksellers, and attached himself to literary pursuits altogether. He married twice. Of his first wife little is known: his second was a sister of Cosway, the painter. She is described to have been an amiable and affectionate woman, who, by her praiseworthy conduct, materially alleviated the distress which his improvidence frequently brought on him. In the year 1806, and for some time after, he was employed on the Times Newspaper.

In 1808 his pecuniary difficulties brought him to the King's Bench, where he passed the last fifteen years of his life, and ultimately died in the year 1823, at about the age of eighty.

He became so enamoured of his confinement, that when, in his latter years, his friends offered to effect an arrangement for his liberation, he declined their assistance, on account of the trouble it would give him; observing, that if he were again at liberty, and established in the most pleasant spot round London, he should only feel perplexed by having to choose his walk.

At that period of advanced life when the weight of years usually bears down the elasticity of the mind, he retained all that spring of intellect which characterized the promptitude of his earlier days, and when infirmities added their load to the pressure of old age, his mental strength still appeared equal to the burthen.

It is singular that a man who wrote so much, and so well, as Mr. COMBE, should not have affixed his name to his productions; but, with the exception of one of the later editions of DR. SYNTAX, they were all published anonymously.

Besides innumerable contributions to periodicals and other works, he wrote Clifton, a Poem—A Satire on Sir James Wright—The Diaboliad, a severe satire on many of the most noted personages of the day—Lord Lyttelton's Letters—The Devil upon Two Sticks in London—History of the Thames—A Letter to the Duchess of Devonshire on Female Education—Letters from an Italian Nun to an English Nobleman, professedly a translation from Rousseau—The Tour of Dr. Syntax in search of the Picturesque—and, stimulated by its extraordinary success, second and third parts to it—Westminster Abbey—History of Oxford—Dance of Death—History of the Public Schools of England—Dance of Life—Johnny Quæ Genus—Amelia's Letters, &c.

In his Diaboliad is an anecdote of an Irish nobleman and his son who quarrelled, and the hatred between them grew so intense, that the father challenged the son to fight a duel. This the latter refused, alleging that he did so, not because the challenger was his father, but because he was not a gentleman.

At about the age of sixty-five he formed an acquaintance with, and was constantly and solely afterwards employed by, the late Mr. ACKERMANN, the money side of whose ledger would, if evidence were wanting, furnish a constructive record of the period of his death; for, as that gentleman significantly observed, "he ceased not to draw till he ceased to breathe." Such was the confidence that subsisted between them, that no contract was ever made as to the price of Mr. COMBE'S labours. "Send me a twenty pounder," or "a thirty pounder," as the want might be, was all that ever passed. He was supplied liberally, his works were profitable, and the publisher satisfied.

The rules of the King's Bench were jocularly asserted, by one of the judges, to reach to the East Indies. In Mr. COMBE'S case they certainly extended to the Strand; for, during the earlier portion of his residence within them, he was a frequent visitor at Mr. ACKERMANN'S table, where, though he manifested considerable epicurism in his eating, his only beverage was water. It was about this time that he wrote those humorous accompaniments to the unrivalled pencil of ROWLANDSON, which assumed the name of "DOCTOR SYNTAX'S TOUR IN SEARCH OF THE PICTURESQUE," and form the subject of the present volume.

List of the Plates.

List of the Plates

TOUR

IN

SEARCH OF THE PICTURESQUE.

CANTO I.

THE School was done, the business o'er,
When tired of Greek and Latin lore,
Good SYNTAX sought his easy chair,
And sat in calm composure there.
His wife was to a neighbour gone,
To hear the chit-chat of the town;
And left him the unfrequent power
Of brooding through a quiet hour.
Thus, while he sat, a busy train
Of images, besieged his brain.
Of Church-preferment he had none;
Nay, all his hope of that was gone:
He felt that he content must be
With drudging in a curacy.
Indeed, on every Sabbath-day,
Through eight long miles he took his way,
To preach, to grumble, and to pray:
To cheer the good, to warn the sinner,
And, if he got it,—eat a dinner:
To bury these, to christen those,
And marry such fond folks as chose

To change the tenor of their life,
And risk the matrimonial strife.
Thus were his weekly journeys made,
'Neath summer suns and wintry shade
And all his gains, it did appear,
Were only thirty pounds a year.
Besides the augmenting taxes press
To aid expense and add distress;
Mutton and beef and bread and beer
And every thing was grown so dear;
The boys too always prone to eat
Delighted less in books than meat;
So that when holy Christmas came,
His earnings ceased to be the same;
And now, alas, could do no more,
Than keep the wolf without the door.
E'en birch, the pedant master's boast,
Was so increased in worth and cost,
That oft, prudentially beguiled
To save the rod, he spared the child.
Thus, if the times refused to mend,
He to his school must put an end.
How hard his lot! how blind his fate!
What shall he do to mend his state?
Thus did poor Syntax ruminate.

When, as the vivid meteors fly,
And instant light the gloomy sky,
A sudden thought across him came,
And told the way to wealth and fame;
And, as the expanding vision grew
Wider and wider to his view,

The painted fancy did beguile
His woe-worn phiz into a smile.
But, while he paced the room around,
Or stood immersed in thought profound,
The Doctor 'midst his rumination,
Was wakened by a visitation
Which troubles many a poor man's life—
The visitation of his wife.
Good Mrs. Syntax was a lady
Ten years, perhaps, beyond her hey-day;
But though the blooming charms had flown
That graced her youth; it still was known
The love of power she never lost,
As Syntax found it to his cost:
For as her words were used to flow,
He but replied, or YES, or NO.—
Whene'er enraged by some disaster,
She'd shake the boys, and cuff the master:
Nay, to avenge the slightest wrong,
She could employ both arms and tongue;
And, if we list to country tales,
She sometimes would enforce her nails.
Her face was red, her form was fat,
A round-about, and rather squat;
And, when in angry humour stalking,
Was like a dumpling set a-walking.
'Twas not the custom of this spouse
To suffer long a quiet house;
She was among those busy wives
Who hurry-scurry through their lives;
And make amends for fading beauty
By telling husbands of their duty.

'Twas at this moment, when, inspired,
And by his new ambition fired,
The pious man his hands upreared,
That Mrs. Syntax re-appeared:
Amazed she looked, and loud she shrieked,
Or, rather like a pig she squeaked,
To see her humble husband dare
Thus quit his sober evening chair,
And pace, with varying steps, about,
Now in the room, and now without.
At first she did not find her tongue,
(A thing which seldom happened long.)
But soon that organ grew unquiet,
To ask the cause of all this riot.
The Doctor smiled, and thus addressed
The secrets of his labouring breast——
"Sit down, my love, my dearest dear,
Nay, prithee do, and patient hear;
Let me, for once, throughout my life,
Receive this kindness from my wife;
It will oblige me so:—in troth,
It will, my dear, oblige us both;
For such a plan has come athwart me,
Which some kind sprite from heaven has brought me,
That, if you will your counsels join,
To aid this golden scheme of mine,
New days will come—new times appear,
And teeming plenty crown the year:
We then on dainty bits shall dine,
And change our home-brewed ale for wine:

On summer days, to take the air,
We'll put our Grizzle to a chair;
While you, in silks and muslins fine,
The grocer's wife shall far outshine,
And neighbouring folks be forced to own,
In this fair town you give the ton."
"Oh! tell me," cried the smiling dame,
"Tell me this golden road to fame:
You charm my heart, you quite delight it."—
"I'll make a TOUR—and then I'll WRITE IT.
You well know what my pen can do,
And I'll employ my pencil too:—
I'll ride and write, and sketch and print,
And thus create a real mint;
I'll prose it here, I'll verse it there,
And picturesque it everywhere.
I'll do what all have done before;
I think I shall—and somewhat more.
At Doctor Pompous give a look;
He made his fortune by a book:
And if my volume does not beat it,
When I return, I'll fry and eat it.
Next week the boys will all go home,
And I shall have a month to come.
My clothes, my cash, my all prepare;
Let Ralph look to the grizzle mare;
Though wondering folks may laugh and scoff,
By this day fortnight I'll be off;
And when old Time a month has run,
Our business, Lovey, will be done.
I will in search of fortune roam,
While you enjoy yourself at home."

The story told, the Doctor eased
Of his grand plan, and Madam pleased,
No pains were spared by night or day
To set him forward on his way:
She trimmed his coat—she mended all
His various clothing, great and small;
And better still, a purse was found
With twenty notes of each a pound.
Thus furnished and in full condition
To prosper in his expedition;
At length the lingering moment came
That gave the dawn of wealth and fame.
Incurious Ralph, exact at four,
Led Grizzle, saddled, to the door;
And soon, with more than common state,
The Doctor stood before the gate.
Behind him was his faithful wife;—
"One more embrace, my dearest life!"
Then his gray palfrey he bestrode,
And gave a nod, and off he rode.
"Good luck! good luck!" she loudly cried,
"Vale! O Vale!" he replied.

CANTO II.

THE farewell ceremony o'er,
Madam went in and banged the door:
No woeful tear bedewed her eye,
Nor did she heave a single sigh;
But soon began her daily trade,
To chide the man and scold the maid;
While Syntax, with his scheme besotted,
Along the village gently trotted.
The folks on daily labour bent,
Whistled and carolled as they went;
But as the Doctor passed along, [song.
Bowed down their heads, and ceased their
He gravely nodded to the people,
Then, looking upwards to the steeple,
He thus, in muttering tones, expressed
The disappointments of his breast.
"That thankless parent, Mother Church,
Has ever left me in the lurch;
And, while so many fools are seen
To strut a Rector or a Dean,
Who live in ease and find good cheer
On every day of every year,
So small her share of true discerning,
She turned her back on all my learning.
I've in her vineyard laboured hard,
And what has been my lean reward?

I've dug the ground, while some rich Vicar
Pressed the ripe grape, and drank the liquor;
I fed the flock, while others eat
The mutton's nice, delicious meat;
I've kept the hive, and made the honey,
While the drones pocketed the money.
But now, on better things intent,
On far more grateful labours bent,
New prospects open to my view:
So, thankless Mother Church, adieu!"
Thus, having said his angry say,
Syntax proceeded on his way.

The morning lark ascends on high,
And with its music greets the sky:
The blackbird whistles, and the thrush
Warbles his wild notes in the bush;
While every hedge and every tree
Resound with vocal minstrelsy.
But Syntax, wrapt in thought profound,
Is deaf to each enlivening sound:
Revolving many a golden scheme,
And yielding to the pleasing dream,
The reins hung loosely from his hand;
While Grizzle, senseless of command,
Unguided paced the road along,
Nor knew if it were right or wrong.
Through the deep vale, and up the hill,
By rapid stream or tinkling rill,
Grizzle her thoughtful master bore,
Who, counting future treasure o'er,

And on his weighty projects bent,
Observed not whither Grizzle went.
Thus did kind Fancy's soothing power
Cheat him of many a fleeting hour;
Nor did he know the pacing Sun
Had half his daily circuit run.
Sweet, airy sprite, that can bestow
A pleasing respite to our woe,
That can corroding care beguile,
And make the woe-worn face to smile!
But ah! too soon the vision passes,
Confounded by a pack of asses!
The donkeys brayed; and lo! the sound
Awaked him from his thought profound;
And as he stared and looked around,
He said—or else he seemed to say—
"I find that I have lost my way.
Oh what a wide expanse I see,
Without a wood, without a tree;
No one at hand, no house is near,
To tell the way, or give good cheer;
For now a sign would be a treat,
To tell us we might drink and eat;
But sure there is not in my sight
The sign of any living wight;
And all around upon this common
I see not either man or woman:
Nor dogs to bark, nor cocks to crow,
Nor sheep to bleat, nor herds to low;
Nay, if these asses did not bray,
And thus some signs of life betray,

I well might think that I were hurled
Into some sad, unpeopled world.
How could I come, misguided wretch!
To where I cannot make a sketch?

Thus as he pondered what to do,
A guide-post rose within his view:
And, when the pleasing shape he spied,
He pricked his steed, and thither hied;
But some unheeding, senseless wight,
Who to fair learning owed a spite,
Had every lettered mark defaced,
Which once its several pointers graced.
The mangled post thus long had stood,
An uninforming piece of wood;
Like other guides, as some folks say,
Who neither lead, nor tell the way.
The Sun, as hot as he was bright,
Had got to his meridian height:
'Twas sultry noon—for not a breath
Of cooling zephyr fanned the heath;
When Syntax cried—"'Tis all in vain
To find my way across the plain;
So here my fortune I will try,
And wait till some one passes by:
Upon that bank awhile I'll sit,
And let poor Grizzle graze a bit;
But, as my time shall not be lost,
I'll make a drawing of the post;
And though a flimsy taste may flout it,
There's something picturesque about it;

'Tis rude and rough, without a gloss,
And is well covered o'er with moss;
And I've a right—(who dares deny it?)
To place yon group of asses by it.
Ay! this will do: and now I'm thinking,
That self-same pond where Grizzle's drinking,
If hither brought 'twould better seem,
And faith I'll turn it to a stream;
I'll make this flat a shaggy ridge,
And o'er the water throw a bridge:
I'll do as other sketchers do—
Put anything into the view;
And any object recollect,
To add a grace, and give effect.
Thus, though from truth I haply err,
The scene preserves its character.
What man of taste my right will doubt,
To put things in, or leave them out?
'Tis more than right, it is a duty,
If we consider landscape beauty:
He ne'er will as an artist shine,
Who copies Nature line by line:
Whoe'er from Nature takes a view,
Must copy and improve it too.
To heighten every work of art,
Fancy should take an active part:
Thus I (which few I think can boast)
Have made a Landscape of a Post.

"So far, so good—but no one passes,
No living creature but these asses;

And, should I sit and hear them bray,
I were as great a beast as they:
So I'll be off; from yonder down
I may, perhaps, descry a town;
Or some tall spire among the trees.
May give my way-worn spirits ease."

Grizzle again he soon bestrode,
And waved his whip and off he rode:
But all around was dingy green,
No spire arose, no town was seen.
At length he reached a beaten road:
How great the joy the sight bestowed!
So on he went in pleasant mood,
And shortly gained a stately wood,
Where the refreshing zephyrs played,
And cooled the air beneath the shade.
Oh! what a change, how great the treat,
To fanning breeze from sultry heat!
But ah! how false is human joy!
When least we think it, ills annoy;
For now, with fierce impetuous rush,
Three ruffians issued from a bush;
One Grizzle stopped, and seized the reins,
While they all threat the Doctor's brains.
Poor Syntax, trembling with affright,
Resists not such superior might,
But yields him to their savage pleasure,
And gives his purse, with all its treasure.
Fearing, howe'er, the Doctor's view
Might be to follow and pursue;

The cunning robbers wisely counted
That he, of course, should be dismounted;
And still that it would safer be,
If he were fastened to a tree.
Thus to a tree they quickly bound him;
The cruel cords went round and round him;
And, having of all power bereft him,
They tied him fast—and then they left him.

CANTO III.

By the road side, within the wood,
In this sad state poor Syntax stood;
His bosom heaved with many a sigh,
And the tears stood in either eye.
What could he do?—he durst not bawl;
His noise the robbers might recall:
The villains might again surround him,
And hang him up where they had bound him.
Sure never was an hapless wight
In more uncomfortable plight;
Nor was this all; his pate was bare,
Unsheltered by one lock of hair;
For when the sturdy robbers took him,
His hat and peruke both forsook him.
The insect world were on the wing,
Whose talent is to buzz and sting;
And soon his bare-worn head they sought,
By instinct led, by nature taught;
And dug their little forks within
The tender texture of his skin.
He raged and roared, but all in vain,
No means he found to ease his pain;
The cords, which to the tree had tied him,
All help from either hand denied him:

He shook his head, he writhed his face
With painful look, with sad grimace,
And thus he spoke his hapless case!

"Ah! miserable man," he cried,
"What perils do my course betide!
In this sad melancholy state,
Must I, alas, impatient wait,
Till some kind soul shall haply find me,
And with his friendly hands unbind me?
Nay, I throughout the night may stay,
'Tis such an unfrequented way:
Though what with hunger, thirst and fright,
I ne'er shall last throughout the night;
And could I e'en these ills survive,
The flies will eat me up alive.
What mad ambition made me roam!
Ah! wherefore did I quit my home!
For there I lived remote from harm:
My meals were good, my house was warm;
And, though I was not free from strife,
With other ills that trouble life,
Yet I had learned full well to bear
The nightly scold, the daily care;
And, after many a season past,
I should have found repose at last:
Fate would have signed my long release,
And Syntax would have died in peace;
Nor thus been robbed, and tied and beaten,
And all alive by insects eaten."

But while he thus at Fate was railing,
And Fortune's angry frown bewailing,

A dog's approaching bark he hears;
'Twas sweet as music to his ears;
And soon a sure relief appears.
For, though it bore that general form,
Which oft at home, foretold a storm,
It now appeared an angel's shape,
That promised him a quick escape:
Nor did La Mancha's valorous Knight
Feel greater pleasure at the sight,
When overwhelmed with love and awe,
His Dulcinea first he saw:
For on two trotting palfreys came,
And each one bore a comely dame:
They started as his form they view;
The horses also started too:
The dog with insult seemed to treat him,
And looked as if he longed to eat him.
In piteous tones he humbly prayed
They'd turn aside, and give him aid;
When each leaped quickly from her steed,
To join in charitable deed.
They drew their knives to cut the noose,
And let the mournful prisoner loose;
With kindest words his fate bewail,
While grateful Syntax tells his tale.
The rustic matrons sooth his grief,
Nor offer, but afford relief:
And, turning from the beaten road,
Their well-lined panniers they unload;
When soon upon the bank appeared
A sight his fainting spirits cheered:

They spread the fare with cheerful grace,
And gave a banquet to the place.
Most haply, too, as they untied him,
He saw his hat and wig beside him:
So, thus bewigged and thus behatted,
Down on the grass the Doctor squatted;
When he uplifted either eye,
With grateful accents to the sky.
"'Tis thus," he humbly said, "we read
In sacred books of heavenly deed:
And thus, I find, in my distress,
The Manna of the Wilderness:
'Tis Hermit's fare; but thanks to Heaven,
And those kind souls, by whom 'tis given."
'Tis true that bread, and curds, and fruit,
Do with the pious Hermit suit;
But Syntax surely was mistaken
To think their meals partake of bacon;
Or that those reverend men regale,
As our good Doctors do—with ale;
And these kind dames, in nothing loth,
Took care that he partook of both.

At length 'twas time to bid adieu,
And each their different way pursue:
A kind farewell, a kiss as kind,
He gave them both with heart and mind:
Then off he trudged, and, as he walked,
Thus to himself the Parson talked.
"'Tis well, I think, it is no worse,
For I have only lost my purse:

With all their cruelty and pains,
The rogues have got but trifling gains;
Poor four-and-four-pence is the measure
Of all their mighty pilfered treasure;
For haply there was no divining
I'd a snug pocket in my lining;
And, thanks to Spousy, every note
Was well sewed up within my coat.
But where is Grizzle?—Never mind her;
I'll have her cried, and soon shall find her."
Thus he pursued the winding way,
Big with the evils of the day:
Though the good Doctor kept in view
The favour of its blessings too.
Nor had he paced it half an hour
Before he saw a parish tower,
And soon, with sore fatigue oppressed,
An Inn received him as its guest.
But still his mind with anxious care,
Pondered upon his wandering mare;
He therefore sent the Bellman round,
To see if Grizzle might be found.

Grizzle, ungrateful to her master,
And careless of his foul disaster,
Left him tied up and took her way,
In hopes to meet with corn or hay;
But, as that did not come to pass,
She sought a meadow full of grass:
The farmer in the meadow found her,
And ordered John, his man, to pound her.

Now John was one of those droll folk,
Who oft take mischief for a joke;
And thought 'twould make the master stare,
When he again beheld his mare,
(Perhaps the Gemman might be shocked)
To find her ready cropped and docked:
At all events, he played his fun:
No sooner was it said than done.
But Grizzle was a patient beast,
And minded nought if she could feast:
Like many others, prone to think
The best of life was meat and drink;
Who feel to-day nor care nor sorrow,
If they are sure to feast to-morrow.
Thus Grizzle, as she paced around
The purlieu of the barren pound,
In hungry mood might seem to neigh—
"If I had water, corn, and hay,
I should not thus my fate bewail,
Nor mourn the loss of ears or tail."

In the mean time securely housed,
The Doctor boozed it, and caroused,
The Hostess spread her fairest cheer,
Her best beef-steak, her strongest beer;
And soothed him with her winning chat,
Of—"Pray eat this—and now take that.
Your Reverence, after all your fright,
Wants meat and drink to set you right."
His Reverence praised the golden rule,
Nor did he let his victuals cool:

And, having drank his liquor out,
He took a turn to look about;—
When to the folks about the door
He told the dismal story o'er.
The country-people on him gazed,
And heard his perils all amazed:
How the thieves twined the cords around him:
How to a tree the villains bound him!
What angels came to his relief,
To loose his bonds, and sooth his grief!
His loss of cash, and what was worse,
His saddle, saddle-bags, and horse.
Thus as their rude attention hung
Upon the wonders of his tongue,
Lo! Grizzle's altered form appears,
With half its tail, and half its ears!
"Is there no law?" the Doctor cries:
"Plenty," a Lawyer straight replies:
"Employ me, and those thieves shall swing
On gallows-tree, in hempen-string:
And, for the rogue, the law shall flea him,
Who maimed your horse, as now you see him."
"No," quoth the Don, "your pardon pray,
I've had enough of thieves to-day:
I've lost four shillings and a groat,
But you would strip me of my coat;
And ears and tail won't fatten you,
You'll want the head and carcase too."
He chuckled as he made the stroke,
And all around enjoyed the joke;
But still it was a sorry sight
To see the beast in such a plight:

Yet what could angry Syntax do?
'Twas all in vain to fret and stew:
His well-stuffed bags, with all their hoard
Of sketching-tools, were safe restored;
The saddle too, which he had sought,
For small reward was quickly brought;
He therefore thought it far more sage
To stop his threats and check his rage;
So to the ostler's faithful care
He gave his mutilated mare;
And while poor Grizzle, free from danger,
Cropped the full rack and cleaned the manger,
Syntax, to ease his aching head,
Smoked out his pipe, and went to bed.

CANTO IV.

BLESS'D be the man, said he of yore
Who Quixote's lance and target bore,
Bless'd be the man who first taught sleep
Throughout our wearied frames to creep,
And kindly gave to human woes
The oblivious mantle of repose!
Hail! balmy power! that canst repair
The constant waste of human care;
To the sad heart afford relief,
And give a respite to its grief;
Canst calm, through night's composing hours,
The threatening storm that daily lowers;
On the rude flint the wretched cheer,
And to a smile transform the tear!

Thus wrapt in slumber, Syntax lay—
Forgot the troubles of the day:
So sound his sleep, so sweet his rest,
By no disturbing dreams distressed;
That, all at ease, he lay entranced,
Till the fair morn was far advanced.
At length, the hostess thought it wrong
He should be left to sleep so long;
So bid the maid to let him know
That breakfast was prepared below.

Betty then oped the chamber door,
And, tripping onwards 'cross the floor,
Undrew the curtains, one by one;
When, in a most ear-piercing tone,
Such as would grace the London cries,
She told him it was time to rise.
The noise his peaceful slumbers broke;
He gave a snort or two—and woke.

Now as the Doctor turned his head,
Betty was curtsying by the bed:
"What brought you here, fair maid, I pray?"
"To tell you, Sir, how wears the day;
And that it is my special care
To get your Worship's morning fare.
The kettle boils, and I can boast
No small renown for making toast.
There's coffee, Sir, and tea, and meat,
And surely you must want to eat;
For ten long hours have passed away
Since down upon this bed you lay!"
The Doctor rubbed his opening eyes,
Then stretched his arms, and 'gan to rise:
But Betty still demurely stands,
To hear him utter his commands.
"Be gone," he cried, "get something nice,
And I'll be with you in a trice."

Behold him then, renewed by rest,
His chin well shaved, his peruke dressed,
Conning with solemn air the news,
His welcome breakfast to amuse;

And when the well-fed meal was o'er,
Grizzle was ordered to the door:
Betty was also told to say,
The mighty sum there was to pay:
Betty, obedient to his will,
Her curtsy makes, and brings the bill.
Down the long page he cast his eye,
Then shook his head, and heaved a sigh.
"What! am I doomed, where'er I go,
In all I meet to find a foe?
Where'er I wander to be cheated,
To be bamboozled and ill treated?"
Thus, as he read each item o'er,
The hostess oped the parlour door;
When Syntax rose in solemn state,
And thus began the fierce debate.

SYNTAX.

"Good woman; here, your bill retake,
And, prithee, some abatement make:
I could not such demands afford,
Were I a Bishop or a Lord:
And though I hold myself as good
As any of my brotherhood,
Howe'er, by bounteous Fortune crowned,
In wealth and honours they abound;
It is not in my power to pay
Such long-drawn bills as well as they.
The paper fills me with affright;—
I surely do not read it right:
For at the bottom here, I see
The enormous total—one pound, three!"

HOSTESS.

"The charges all are fairly made;
If you will eat, I must be paid.
My bills have never found reproaches
From Lords and Ladies, in their coaches.
This house that's called the Royal Crown,
Is the first Inn throughout the town:
The best of gentry, every day,
Become my guests, and freely pay:
Besides, I took you in at night,
Half dead with hunger and affright,
Just 'scaped from robbers."

SYNTAX.

. . . . "That's most true,
And now I'm to be robbed by you."

HOSTESS.

"Sir, you mistake; and did not I
Disdain rude words, I'd say—you lie.
I took you in last night, I say."—

SYNTAX.

"'Tis true;—and if this bill I pay,
You'll *take me in* again to-day."

HOSTESS.

"I gave you all my choicest cheer,
The best of meat, the best of beer;
And then you snored yourself to rest
In the best bed—I say the best.
You've had such tea as few can boast,
With a whole loaf turned into toast."

SYNTAX.

"And for your beef, and beer and tea,
You kindly charge me—one pound three!"

HOSTESS.

"'Tis cheap as dirt—for well I know
How things with country Curates go:
And I profess that I am loth
To deal unkindly with the cloth:
Nay, oft and oft, as I'm a sinner,
I've given hungry Clerks a dinner."

SYNTAX.

"And there's a proverb, as they say,
That for the Clerks the Parsons pay;
Which you, I trow, can well fulfil,
Whene'er you make a Parson's bill.
Why, one pound three, the truth I speak,
Would keep my household for a week.
Dear Mrs. Syntax how she'd vapour
Were she to read this curious paper!"

HOSTESS.

"If that's your living, on my life,
You starve your servants and your wife."

SYNTAX.

"I wish my wife were here to meet you,
In your own fashion she would greet you:
With looks as fierce, and voice as shrill,
She'd make you, mistress, change your bill."

HOSTESS.

"Think you, besides, there's nought to pay
For all your horse's corn and hay?

And ointments too, to cure the ail
Of her cropped ears and mangled tail?"

SYNTAX.

"I wish the wight would bring the shears
Which docked that tail and cropped those ears,
And just exert the self-same skill
To crop and dock your monstrous bill!
But, I'm in haste to get away,
Though one pound three I will not pay:
So, if you'll take one half the amount,
We'll quickly settle the account.
There is your money, do you see?
And let us part in charity."

HOSTESS.

"Well, as a charitable deed,
I'll e'en consent—so mount your steed,
And on your journey straight proceed:
But well you know, where'er you roam,
That Charity begins at home."

CANTO V.

The Doctor smiled, the bill was paid,
The hostess left him to the maid;
When Betty stood in humble guise,
With expectation in her eyes,
That he was surely so good-hearted,
To give her something ere they parted.
Now, Nature in her wanton freaks,
Had given Betty rosy cheeks;
And caused her raven locks to break
In native ringlets on her neck:
The roving bee might wish to sip
The sweetness of her pouting lip;
So red, so tempting to the view,
'Twas what the Doctor longed to do.
"You're a nice girl," he smiling said.
"Am I?" replied the simpering maid.
"I swear you are, and if you're willing
To give a kiss, I'll give a shilling."
"If 'tis the same thing, Sir, to you,
Make the gift two-fold, and take two."
He grimly grinned with inward pleasure,
And instant seized the purchased treasure.
"Your lips, my dear, are sweet as honey:
So one smack more—and there's your money."

This charming ceremony o'er,
The Parson strutted to the door;

Where his poor wounded mare appears
In cruel state of tail and ears.
The neighbours all impatient wait
To see him issue from the gate;
For country-town or village-green
Had seldom such a figure seen.
Labour stood still to see him pass,
While every lad and every lass
Ran forward to enjoy the feast,
To jeer the Sage, and mourn the beast.
But one and all, aloud declare,
'Twas a fit sight for country-fair;
Far better than a dancing bear.

At length, escaped from all the noise
Of women, men, and girls and boys,
In the recesses of a lane
He thus gave utterance to his pain.
"It seems to be my luckless case,
At every point, in every place,
To meet with trouble and disgrace.
But yesterday I left my home,
In search of fancied wealth to roam;
And nought, I think, but ills betide me
Sure some foul spirit runs beside me:
Some blasting demon from the east,
A deadly foe to man and beast,
That loves to riot in disaster,
And plague alike both horse and master.
Grizzle, who full five years, and more,
A trumpeter in triumph bore;

Who had in hard-fought battle been,
And many a bloody conflict seen;
Who, having 'scaped with scarce a scar,
'Mid all the angry threats of war;
When her best days are almost past,
Feels these ignoble wounds at last.
Ah! what can thy fond master do,
He's cut and slashed as well as you!
But, though no more with housing gay,
And prancing step you take your way;
Or, with your stately rider, lead
The armed troop to warlike deed;
While you've a leg, you ne'er shall cease
To bear the minister of peace.
Long have you borne him nor e'er grumbled,
Nor ever started, kicked or stumbled."

But mildest natures sometimes err
From the strict rules of character:
The timorous bird defends it's young,
And beasts will kick when they are stung.
'Twas burning hot, and hosts of flies,
With venomed stings, around them rise:
They seized on Grizzle's wounded part,
Who straight began to snort and start;
Kicked up behind, reared up before,
And played a dozen antics more:
The Doctor coaxed, but all in vain,
She snorted, kicked, and reared again:
"Alas!" said Syntax, "could I pop
Just now, upon a blacksmith's shop,

Whose cooling unguents would avail
To save poor Grizzle's ears and tail!"
When scarce had he his wishes spoke,
Than he beheld a cloud of smoke,
That from a forge appeared to rise,
And for a moment veiled the skies;
While the rude hammers to his ear,
Proclaimed the aid he wished was near.
By the way-side the cottage rose,
Around it many a willow grows,
Where Syntax in a tone of grief,
Showed Grizzle's wounds and prayed relief.
The sooty Galen soon appeared,
And with fair hopes the Doctor cheered.
"Trust me, good Sir, I've got a plaster,
Will cure the beast of her disaster;
And while the dressing I prepare,
With all becoming skill and care,
You in that arbour may regale
With a cool pipe and jug of ale:
I've long a two-fold trade professed,
And med'cine sell for man and beast."
—Syntax now sought the cooling shade,
While Galen's dame the banquet made:
She well knew how her guests to please,
And added meat, and bread and cheese:
Besides, she told the village-tale—
Who came to drink her home-brewed ale;
How that the laughter-loving Vicar
Would sometimes walk to taste their liquor;
That their gay landlord was renowned,
For hunting fox, with horn and hound;

That he'd a daughter passing fair,
Who was his Honour's only heir;
But she was proud, nor could a 'Squire
Approach to tell his amorous fire;
A Lord alone, as it was said,
She would receive into her bed.
Throughout the village, every name
Became a subject for the dame;
And thus she played her chattering part,
Till Syntax thought it time to start.
And now poor Grizzle reappears,
With plastered tail and plastered ears,
Which thus cased up, might well defy
The sharpest sting of gnat or fly.
The Doctor having had his fill,
Without a word discharged his bill:
But, as it was the close of day,
He trotted briskly on his way;
And ere the sun withdrew his light
An Inn received him for the night.
His frame fatigued, his mind oppressed,
He tiffed his punch, and went to rest.
The morning came, when he arose
In spirits from his calm repose;
And while the maid prepared the tea,
He looked around the room to see
What story did the walls disclose,
Of human joys, of human woes.
The window quickly caught his eye,
On whose clear panes he could descry
The motley words of many a Muse:
There was enough to pick and choose;

And, "Faith," said he, "I'll strive to hook
Some of these lines into my book:
For here there are both grave and witty,
And some, I see, are rather pretty."
From a small pocket in his coat
He drew his tablets,—when he wrote
Whate'er the pregnant panes possessed;
And these choice lays among the rest.

"If my fond breast were made of glass,
And you could see what there doth pass,
Kitty, my ever charming fair!
You'd see your own sweet image there."

"I once came here a free-booting,
And on this fine manor went shooting,
And if the 'Squire this truth denies,
This glass shall tell the 'Squire—he lies."

"Dolly's as fat as any sow,
And, if I'm not mistaken,
Dolly is well disposed, I trow,
To trim her husband's bacon."

"Dear Jenny, while your name I hear,
No transient glow my bosom heats;
And when I meet your eye, my dear,
My fluttering heart no longer beats.
I dream, but I no longer find
Your form still present to my view;
I wake, but now my vacant mind
No longer waking dreams of you.

I can find maids, in every rout,
With smiles as false and forms as fine;
But you must hunt the world throughout,
To find a heart as true as mine."

"I hither came down
From fair London town
With Lucy, so mild and so kind;
But Lucy grew cool,
And called me a fool,
So I started and left her behind."

But as he copied, quite delighted,
All that the Muse had thus indited,
A hungry dog, and prone to steal,
Ran off with half his breakfast meal;
While Dolly, entering with a kettle,
Was followed by a man of mettle,
Who swore he'd have the promised kiss;
And, as he seized the melting bliss,
From the hot, ill-poised kettle's spout,
The boiling stream came pouring out,
And drove the Doctor from the Muse,
By quickly filling both his shoes.

CANTO VI.

WHAT various evils man await,
In this strange, sublunary state!
No sooner is he cheered by joy,
Than sorrows come, and pains annoy;
And scarce his lips are oped to bless
The transient gleam of happiness,
Than some dark cloud obscures the sky,
And grief's sad moisture fills his eye.

Thus, while the Doctor smiling stol
From the clear glass each witty scroll,
He felt, to interrupt the treat,
The scalding torment in his feet:
And, thus awakened from his trance,
Began to skip, and jump, and dance.
"Take off my shoes," he raving cried,
"And let my gaiters be untied."
When Dolly with her nimble hand,
Instant obeyed the loud command;
And, as he lolled upon the chair,
His feet and ankles soon were bare.
Away the impatient damsel run,
To cure the mischief she had done;
And quick returned with liquid store,
To rub his feet and ankles o'er:

Nor was the tender office vain,
That soon assuaged the burning pain.
A tear was seen on Dolly's cheek;
Who sighed as if her heart would break.
" Be not, my girl, with care oppressed;
I'm now," says Syntax, "quite at rest:
My anger's vanished with the pain;
No more, my dear, shall I complain,
Since to get rid of my disaster,
So fair a maid presents the plaster."
Thus did he Dolly's care beguile,
And turned her tears into a smile:
But, while she cooled the raging part,
She somehow warmed the Doctor's heart;
And, as she rubbed the ointment in,
He pinched her cheeks and chucked her chin;
And, when she had re-dressed his shanks,
He with a kiss bestowed his thanks:
While gentle Dolly, nothing loth,
Consenting smiled, and took them both.
"I think," said she, "you'd better stay,
Nor travel further on to-day:"—
And though she said it with a smile
His steady purpose to beguile,
The Doctor closed the kind debate,
By ordering Grizzle to the gate.

Now, undisturbed, he took his way,
And travelled till the close of day;
When, to delight his wearied eyes,
Before him Oxford's towers arise.

"O, Alma Mater!" Syntax cried,
"My present boast, my early pride;
To whose protecting care I owe
All I've forgot, and all I know.
Deign from your nursling to receive
The homage that his heart can give.
Hail! sacred, ever-honoured shades
Where oft I wooed the immortal maids;
Where strolling oft, at break of day,
My feet have brushed the dews away!
By Isis and by Cherwell's stream,
How oft I wove the classic dream,
Or sought the cloisters dim, to meet
Pale Science in her lone retreat!
The sight of you, again inspires
My bosom with its former fires:
I feel again the genial glow
That makes me half forget the woe,
And all my aching heart could tell,
Since last I bid these scenes farewell."

Thus Syntax moved in sober pace,
Beset with academic grace;
While Grizzle bore him up the town,
And at the Mitre set him down.
The night was passed in sound repose,
And as the clock struck nine he rose.
The barber now applies his art,
To shave him clean, and make him smart.
From him he learned that Dicky Bend,
His early academic friend,

As a reward for all his knowledge,
Was made the Provost of his College;
And fame declared that he had clear
At least twelve hundred pounds a year.
"O ho!" says Syntax, "if that's true,
I cannot surely better do
Than further progress to delay,
And with Friend Dicky pass a day."
Away he hied, and soon he found him,
With all his many comforts round him.
The Provost hailed the happy meeting,
And, after kind and mutual greeting,
To make inquiries he began;—
And thus the conversation ran.

PROVOST.

"Good Doctor Syntax, I rejoice
Once more to hear your well-known voice;
To dine with us I hope you'll stay,
And share a college feast to-day.
Full many a year is gone and past
Since we beheld each other last:
Fortune has kindly dealt with me,
As you, my friend, may plainly see;
And pray how has she dealt with thee?'

SYNTAX.

"Alas! alas! I've played the fool;
I took a wife and kept a school;
And while on dainties you are fed,
I scarce get butter to my bread."

PROVOST.

"For my part, I have never married,
And grieve to hear your plans miscarried:
I hope then, my old worthy friend,
Your visit here your fate will mend.
My services you may command;—
I offer them with heart and hand;
And while you think it right to stay,
You'll make this house your home I pray."

SYNTAX.

"I'm going further, on a scheme,
Which you may think an idle dream;
At the famed Lakes to take a look,
And of my Journey make a Book."

PROVOST.

"I know full well that you have store
Of modern as of classic lore:
And, surely, with your weight of learning,
And all your critical discerning,
You might produce a work of name,
To fill your purse and give you fame.
How oft have we together sought
Whate'er the ancient sages taught!"

SYNTAX.

"I now perceive that all your knowledge
Is pent, my friend, within your college!
Learning's become a very bore—
That fashion long since has been o'er.
A Bookseller may keep his carriage,
And ask ten thousand pounds in marriage;

May have his mansion in a square,
And build a house for country air;
And yet 'tis odds the fellow knows
If Horace wrote in verse or prose.
Could Doctor G—— in chariot ride,
And take each day his wine beside,
If he did not contrive to cook,
Each year, his Tour into a book;
A flippant, flashy, flowery style,
A lazy morning to beguile;
With ev'ry other leaf, a print
Of some fine view in aquatint?
Such is the book I mean to make,
And I've no doubt the work will take:
For though your wisdom may decry it,
The simple folk will surely buy it.
I will allow it is but trash,
But then it furnishes the cash."

PROVOST.

"Why things are not the same, I fear,
As when we both were scholars here;
But still I doubt not your success,
And wish you every happiness;
Myself, and my whole college tribe,
Depend upon it will subscribe."

At length the bell began to call
To dinner in the college-hall;
Nor did the guests delay to meet,
Lured by the bounty of the treat.
The formal salutations over,
Each drew his chair and seized his cover:

The Provost, in collegiate pride,
Placed Doctor Syntax by his side;
And soon they heard the hurrying feet
Of those that bore the smoking meat.

Behold the dishes due appear—
Fish in the van, beef in the rear;
But he who the procession led,
By some false step or awkward tread,
Or cursed by some malignant power,
Fell headlong on the marble floor!
Ah, heedless wight! ah, hapless dish!
Ah! all the luxury of fish!
Thus in a moment spoiled and wasted;
Ah! never, never to be tasted!
But one false step begets another,
So they all tumbled one o'er t'other:
And now the pavement was bestrewed
With roast and boiled, and fried and stewed.
The waiters squalled, their backs bespattered
With scalding sauce; the dishes clattered
In various discord; while the brawl
Re-echoed through the astonished hall.
"Well," said a Don, "as I'm a sinner,
We must go elsewhere for a dinner."
"'Tis no such thing," the Head replied,
"You all shall soon be satisfied:
We are but ten: and sure there's plenty;
I ordered full enough for twenty.
I see, my friends, the haunch unspoiled,
With chicken roast, and turkey boiled;

The ven'son pasty is secure,
The marrow puddings safe and sure;
With ham, and many good things more,
And tarts, and custards, full a score.
Sure, here's enough to cut and carve:
To-day, I think, we shall not starve:
But still I'll make the boobies pay
For the good things they've thrown away."
Thus every eye was quickly cheered
With all the plenty that appeared;
They eat, they drank, they smoked, they talked,
And round the college-garden walked:
But the time came (for time will fly)
When Syntax was to say—"good bye."
His tongue could scarce his feeling tell,
Could scarce pronounce the word, "farewell!"
The Provost too, whose generous heart
In those same feelings bore a part,
Told him, when he should want a friend
To write, or come, to Dicky Bend.
Next morning, at an early hour,
Syntax proceeded on his Tour;
And as he sauntered on his way,
The scene of many a youthful day,
He thought 'twould give his book an air,
If Oxford were well painted there:
And, as he curious looked around,
He saw a spot of rising ground,
From whence the turrets of the city
Would make a picture very pretty:
Where Radcliff's dome would intervene,
And Magd'len tower crown the scene.

So Grizzle to a hedge he tied,
And onward then impatient hied;
But, as he sought to choose a part
Where he might best display his art,
A wicked bull no sooner viewed him,
Than loud he roared, and straight púrsued him.
The Doctor finding danger near,
Flew swiftly on the wings of fear,
And nimbly clambered up a tree,
That gave him full security;
But as he ran to save his bacon,
By hat and wig he was forsaken;
His sketch-book too he left behind,
A prey to the unlucky wind:
While Grizzle, startled by the rout,
Broke from the hedge, and pranced about.
Syntax, still trembling with affright,
Clung to the tree with all his might;
He called for help—and help was near,
For dogs, and men, and boys appear:
So that his foe was forced to yield,
And leave him master of the field.
No more of roaring bulls afraid,
He left the tree's protecting shade;
And as he paced the meadow round,
His hat, his wig, his book he found.
"Come, my old girl," the Doctor said,
The faithful steed the call obeyed.
So Grizzle once more he bestrode,
Nor looked behind—but off he rode.

CANTO VII.

FIXED in cogitation deep,
Adown the hill and up the steep,
Along the moor and through the wood,
Syntax his pensive way pursued:
And now his thoughts began to roam,
To the good woman left at home;
How she employed the passing day
When her fond mate was far away·
For they possessed, with all their pother,
A sneaking kindness for each other.
Proud of her husband's stock of learning,
His classic skill and deep discerning,
No tongue she suffered to dethrone
His fond importance—but her own.
Besides, she was a very bee
In bustle and in industry;
And though a pointed sting she bore,
That sometimes made the Doctor sore,
She helped to make the household thrive,
And brought home honey to the hive.
He too had not forgot her charms,
When first he took her to his arms;
For, if report relates the truth,
She was a beauty in her youth:
The charming Dolly was well known
To be the toast of all the town;

And, though full many a year was gone,
Since this good dame was twenty-one,
She still retained the air and mien
Of the nice girl she once had been.
For these and other charms beside,
She was indeed the Doctor's pride;
Nay, he would sometimes on her gaze
With the fond looks of former days;
And, whatsoe'er she did or said,
He kept his silence and obeyed.
Besides, his mind he thus consoled;
"'Tis classical to be a scold;
For, as the ancient tomes record,
Zantippe's tongue was like a sword:
She was about my Dolly's age,
And the known helpmate of a sage.
Thus Socrates, in days of yore,
The self-same persecution bore:
Nor shall I blush to share the fate
Of one so good—of one so great."

'Twas now five days since they had parted,
And he was ever tender-hearted:
Whene'er he heard the wretched sigh
He felt a Christian sympathy;
For though he played the demi-god
Among his boys, with rule and rod;
What though he spoke in pompous phrase,
And kept the vulgar in amaze;
Though self-important he would stride
Along the street with priestly pride;

Though his strange figure would provoke
The passing smile, the passing joke;
Among the high, or with the low,
Syntax had never made a foe;
And, though the jest of all he knew,
Yet, while they laughed they loved him too:
No wonder then, so far from home,
His head would shake, the sigh would come.
Thus he went gently on his way,
Till the sun marked declining day.

But Thought as well as grief is dry,
And, lo! a friendly cot was nigh,
Whose sign, high dangling in the air,
Invites the traveller to repair,
Where he in comfort may regale,
With cooling pipe and foaming ale.
The Doctor gave the loud command,
And sees the Host beside him stand;
Then quits his steed with usual state,
And passes through the wicket-gate;
The Hostess opes the willing door,
And then recounts the humble store
Which her poor cottage could afford,
To place upon the frugal board.
The homespun napkin soon was laid,
The table all its ware displayed:
The well-broiled rasher then appeared,
And with fresh eggs his stomach cheered;
The crusty pie, with apples lined,
Sweetened the feast on which he dined,

And liquor, that was brewed at home,
Among the rest was seen to foam.
The Doctor drank—the Doctor eat,
Well pleased to find so fair a treat;
Then to his pipe he kindly took,
And with a condescending look,
Called on the Hostess to relate
What was the village name and state;
And to whose office it was given
To teach them all the way to Heaven.

HOSTESS.

The land belongs to 'Squire Bounty,
No better man lives in the county:
I wish the Rector were the same;
One Doctor Squees'em is his name;
But we ne'er see him—more's the shame.
And while in wealth he cuts and carves,
The worthy Curate prays and starves.

SYNTAX.

I truly wish that he were here
To take a pipe and share my beer;
I know what 'tis as well as he,
To serve a man I never see.

Just as he spoke, the Curate came:—
"This, this is he!" exclaimed the dame.
Syntax his brother Parson greeted,
And begged him to be quickly seated;
"Come, take a pipe, and taste the liquor,
'Tis good enough for any Vicar."

CURATE.

Alas! Sir, I'm no Vicar;—I,
Bound to an humble Curacy,
With all my care can scarce contrive
To keep my family alive.
While the fat Rector can afford
To eat and drink like any Lord:
But know, Sir, I'm a man of letters,
And ne'er speak evil of my betters.

SYNTAX.

That's good;—but when we suffer pain,
'Tis Nature's office to complain;
And when the strong oppress the weak,
Justice, though blind, will always speak.
Tell me, have you explained your case,
With due humility and grace?
The great and wealthy must be flattered,
They love with praise to be bespattered:
Indeed, I cannot see the harm,
If thus you can their favour charm;
If by fine phrases you can bend
The pride of Power to be your friend.

CURATE.

I wrote, I'm sure, in humblest style,
And praised his goodness all the while:
I begged, as things had grown so dear,
He'd raise my pay ten pounds a year;
And, as I now had children five,
The finest little bairns alive,
While their poor, fond and faithful mother
Would soon present me with another;

And, as the living brought him, clear,
At least a thousand pounds a year,
He'd grant the favour I implore,
Nor let me starve upon threescore.

SYNTAX.

Now I should like without delay,
To hear what this rich man could say;
For I can well perceive, my friend,
That you did not obtain your end.

CURATE.

The postman soon a letter brought,
Which cost me six-pence and a groat:
Nor can your friendly heart suggest
The rudeness which the page expressed.
"Such suits as yours may well miscarry,
For beggars should not dare to marry;
At least, for I will not deceive you,
I never, never will relieve you;
And if you trouble me, be sure
You shall be ousted from the Cure."
But I shall now, good Sir, refrain,
Because I know 'twould give you pain,
From telling all that in his spite,
The arch old scoundrel chose to write;
For know, Sir, I'm a man of letters,
And never will abuse my betters.

SYNTAX.

Zounds!—'tis enough to make one swear,
Nor can I such a monster bear:
But think, my friend, on that great day
Of strict account, when he must pay

For all his cruelty and lies:—
Then he shall sink, and you will rise.

CURATE.

The terms, I own, are not quite civil,
But he's the offspring of the devil;
And, when the day of life is past,
He'll with his father dwell at last.
But know, Sir, I'm a man of letters,
And ne'er wish evil to my betters.

'Twas thus they talked and drank their ale,
Till the dim shades of eve prevail;
When Syntax settled each demand:
And, while he held the Curate's hand,
Bid him be stout and not despair:
"The poor are God's peculiar care:
You're not the only one, my friend,
Who has with evil to contend:
Resign yourself to what is given:
Be good, and leave the rest to Heaven."
Syntax, we've said, was tender hearted·—
He dropped a tear, and then departed.

The evening lowered,—a drizzly rain
Had spread a mist o'er all the plain;
Besides the home-brewed beer began
To prey upon the inward man:
And Syntax, muddled, did not know
Or where he was, or where to go.

An active horseman by him trotted,
And Syntax was not so besotted

But he could hiccup out, "My friend,
Do tell me if this way will tend
To bring me to some place of rest?"
"Yes," 'twas replied,—"the very best
Of all our inns, within a mile,
Will soon your weariness beguile."
Who should this be but 'Squire Bounty,
So much beloved throughout the county,
And he resolved, by way of jest,
To have the Parson for his guest;
So on he gallopped, to prepare
His people for the friendly snare.
The Doctor came in tipsy state;
The 'Squire received him at the gate,
And to a parlour led him straight;
Then placed him in an easy chair,
And asked to know his pleasure there.

SYNTAX.

Landlord, I'm sadly splashed with mire
And chilled with rain, so light a fire;
And tell the Ostler to take care
Of that good beast, my grizzle mare;
And what your larder can afford,
Pray place it quickly on the board.

'SQUIRE.

We've butcher's meat, of every kind;
But, if that is not to your mind,
There's poultry, Sir, and if you please,
Our cook excels in fricassees.

SYNTAX.

Tell me, my honest friend, I pray,
What kind of fowl or fish are they?
Besides, my very civil Host,
I wish to know what they will cost;
For a poor Parson can't afford
To live on dainties like a Lord.

'SQUIRE.

The Clergy, Sir, when here they stay,
Are never, never asked to pay:
I love the Church, and, for its sake,
I ne'er make bills or reckonings take;
Proud if its ministers receive
The little that I have to give.

SYNTAX.

Why, then, my friend, you're never dull;
Your inn, I trow, is always full:—
'Tis a good rule, must be confest,
But, though I blink, I see a jest.

'SQUIRE.

No, Sir; you see the cloth is laid,
And not a farthing to be paid.

SYNTAX.

I find my head's not very clear;
My eyes see double too, I fear;
For all these things can never be
Prepared for such a guest as me:
A banquet it must be allowed,
Of which Olympus might be proud.

Thus Syntax eat and drank his fill,
Regardless of the morrow's bill;
He rang the bell, and called the waiters,
To rid him of his shoes and gaiters.
"Go tell the maid to show the bed,
Where I may lay my aching head;
Here, take my wig, and bring a cap;
My eye-lids languish for a nap:
No curtsying pray; I want no fawning,
For I shall break my jaws with yawning."
Now, Kitty, to adorn his crown,
Brought him a night-cap of her own;
And, having put it on, she bound it
With a pink ribbon round and round it.
In this fine guise was Syntax led
Up the best stairs, and put to bed.
Though mirth prevailed the house throughout,
Though it was all one revel rout,
He heard it not, nor did he know
The merriment he caused below;
For, with fatigue and wine oppressed,
He grunted, groaned, and went to rest.
But when the sun in Thetis' lap,
Had taken out his usual nap,
Syntax awoke, and, looking 'round,
The sight his senses did confound.
He saw that he had laid his head
Within a fine-wrought silken bed:
A gaudy carpet graced the floor,
And gilded mouldings decked the door,
Nor did the mirror fail to show
His own sweet form from top to toe.

"If I," said he, "remember right,
I was most lordly drunk last night:
And, as the Tinker in the play
Was taken, when dead-drunk he lay,
And made a lord for half a day;
I think that some one has made free
To play the self-same trick with me:
But I'll contrive to be possessed
Of this same secret when I'm dressed:
To find it out I'll ring the bell;
The chamber-maid the truth may tell."
She soon appeared, and curtsying low,
Requested his commands to know.—
"When and how did I come here?
You'll be so good to say, my dear."
"—You came last night, not very late,
About the time the clock struck eight;
And I have heard the servants say,
They thought that you had lost your way."
"—Inform me also, how you call
This noble inn?" "'Tis Welcome Hall."
"And pray who have you in the house?"
"We've 'Squire Bounty and his spouse;
With Lady and Sir William Hearty,
And you, good Sir, may join the party:
Indeed, I'm ordered to request
That you will be their morning guest."

To question more he did not stay,
But bid the damsel show the way.
O! 'twas a very pleasant meeting:
The Landlord gave a hearty greeting,

And placed the Doctor in a chair,
Between two Ladies, young and fair.
Syntax, well pleased, began to prate,
And all his history to relate;
While mirth and laughter loud prevail,
As he let forth the curious tale.
At length the 'Squire explained the joke:
When thus the Doctor quaintly spoke:—
"I beg, Sir, no excuse you'll make,
Your merriment I kindly take;
And only wish the gods would give
Such jesting every day I live."

The ladies pressed his longer stay,
But Syntax said—he must away:
So Grizzle soon her master bore,
Some new adventure to explore.

CANTO VIII.

"In every way, in every sense,
Man is the care of Providence;
And whensoe'er he goeth wrong,
The errors to himself belong;
Nor do we always judge aright
Of Fortune's favours, or her spite.
How oft with pleasure we pursue
Some glittering phantom in our view;
Not rightly seen or understood,
We chase it as a real good:
At length the air-born vision flies,
And each fond expectation dies!
Sometimes the clouds appear to lower,
And threat misfortune's direful hour:
We tremble at the approaching blast:
Each hope is fled—we look aghast;
When lo! the darkness disappears,
The glowing sun all nature cheers;
The drooping heart again acquires
Its former joys, its former fires.
Last night I wandered o'er the plain,
Through unknown ways and beating rain
Nor thought 'twould be my lot to fall
On such an inn as Welcome Hall;

Indeed with truth I cannot say
When there I came I lost my way,
For all was good, and nought to pay."

Thus Syntax, with reflection fraught,
Soliloquized the moral thought;
While Grizzle, all alive and gay,
Ambled along the ready way.
Last night she found it no disaster
To share the fortune of her master;
She 'mong the finest hunters stood,
And shared with them the choicest food:
In a fine roomy stable placed,
With every well-trimmed clothing graced,
Poor Grizzle was as fair a joke
To all the merry stable-folk,
As the good Doctor's self had been
To the kind gentry of the Inn.

Enrapt in Contemplation's power,
Syntax forgot the fleeting hour;
Till looking round he saw the sun
Had passed his bright meridian run.
A shepherd-boy he now espied,
Strolling along the highway side;
And, on his wandering flock intent,
The stripling whistled as he went.
"My honest lad, perhaps you know
What distance I shall have to go,
Before my eager eyes may greet
Some place where I may drink and eat."

"Continue, master, o'er the Down,
And soon you'll reach the neighbouring town:
In less, I think, than half an hour,
You'll pass by yonder lofty tower:
Keep onward by the church-yard wall,
And you will see an house of call;
The sign's a Dragon—there you'll find
Eating and drinking to your mind."
Across the Down the Doctor went,
And towards the church his way he bent.
"Thus," Syntax said, "when man is hurled
Upwards and downwards in the world;
When some strong impulse makes him stray
From Virtue's path to Folly's way,
The Church,—Religion's holy seat,
Will guide to peace his wandering feet!
But, hark! the death-bell's solemn toll
Tells the departure of a soul;
The Sexton too I see prepares
The place where end all human cares.
And, lo, a crowd of tombs appear!
I may find something curious here;
For oft poetic flowers are found
To flourish in sepulchral ground.
I'll just walk in and take a look,
And pick up matter for my book:
The living, some wise man has said,
Delight in reading of the dead.
What golden gains my book would boast,
If I could meet a chatty ghost,
Who would some news communicate
Of its unknown and present state:

Some pallid figure in a shroud,
Or sitting on a murky cloud;
Or kicking up a new-made grave,
And screaming forth some horrid stave;
Or bursting from the hollow tomb,
To tell of bloody deeds to come;
Or adverse skeletons embattling,
With ghastly grins and bones a rattling;
Something to make the misses stare,
And force upright their curly hair;
To cause their pretty forms to shake,
And make them doubt if they're awake:
And thus to tonnish folks present
The Picturesque of Sentiment!
But 'tis, I fear, some hours too soon—
Ghosts slumber all the afternoon:
I'll ask the Sexton if, at night,
I may perchance pick up a sprite."

The Doctor in canonic state,
Now oped at once the church-yard gate;
While Grizzle too thought fit to pass,
Who knew the taste of church-yard grass.
"Sir," cried the Sexton, "let me say,
That you must take your mare away,
Or else, believe me, I am bound
To lead her quickly to the pound."

"You do mistake, my honest friend—
'Tis a foul wrong that you intend.
A Parson's mare will claim a right
In a church-yard to take a bite;

And, as I come to meditate
Among these signs of human fate,
I beg you will not make a riot,
But let the poor beast feed in quiet."
No more the conscious Sexton said,
But urged his labours for the dead;
While Syntax culled, with critic care,
What the sad muse had written there.

EPITAPHS.

Here lies poor Thomas and his wife,
Who led a pretty jarring life;
But all is ended, do you see?
He holds his tongue, and so does she.

If drugs and physic could but save
Us mortals from the dreary grave,
'Tis known that I took full enough
Of the Apothecary's stuff,
To have prolonged life's busy feast
To a full century at least;
But, spite of all the Doctor's skill,
Of daily draught and nightly pill,
Reader, as sure as you're alive,
I was sent here at twenty-five.

Within this tomb a lover lies,
Who fell an early sacrifice
To Dolly's unrelenting eyes.
For Dolly's charms poor Damon burned—
Disdain the cruel maid returned:

But, as she danced in May-day pride,
Dolly fell down, and Dolly died,
And now she lays by Damon's side.
Be not hard-hearted then, ye fair!
Of Dolly's hapless fate beware!
For sure, you'd better go to bed
To one alive, than one who's dead.

Beneath the sod the soldier sleeps,
  Whom cruel war refused to spare;
Beside his grave the maiden weeps,
  And Glory plants the laurel there.
Honour is the warrior's meed,
  Or spared to live or doomed to die;
Whether 'tis his lot to bleed,
  Or join the shout of Victory;
Alike the laurel to the truly brave;
That binds the brow, or consecrates the
    grave.

Beneath this stone her ashes rest,
Whose memory fills my aching breast!
She sleeps unconscious of the tear
That tells the tale of sorrow here;
But still the hope allays my pain
That we may meet and love again;
Love with a pure seraphic fire,
That never, never, shall expire.

Syntax the Sexton now addressed,
As on his spade he leaned to rest.

SYNTAX.

"We both, my friend, pursue one trade:
I for the living, you the dead.
For whom that grave do you prepare
With such keen haste, and cheerful air?'

SEXTON.

"An' please your Reverence, Lawyer Thrust,
Thank Heaven, will moulder here to dust:
Never before did I take measure
Of any grave with half the pleasure;
And when within this hole he's laid,
I'll ram the earth down with my spade:
I'll take good care he shall not rise,
Till summoned to the last assize;
And, when he sues for Heaven's grace,
I would not wish to take his place.
He once on cruel deed intent,
Seized on my goods for want of rent;
Nay, I declare, as I'm a sinner,
He took away the children's dinner:
For, as they sat around the table,
Eating as fast as they were able,
He seized the dishes great and small,
The children's bread and milk, and all;
The urchins cried, the mother prayed,
I begged his rigour might be stayed
Till I could on our Parson call,
Who would engage to pay it all;
But he disdained a Parson's word,
And mocked the suit which I preferred.

He knew a better way to thrive;
To pay two pounds by taking five.
Bursting with rage, I knocked him down,
And broke the cruel rascal's crown;
For which in county-gaol I lay,
Half-starving many a bitter day.
But our good Parson brought relief,
And kindly soothed a mother's grief:
He, while in prison I remained,
My little family sustained;
And when I was from durance free,
Made me his Sexton, as you see.
But Doctor Worthy, he is gone;—
You'll read his virtues on the stone
That's placed aloft upon the wall,
Where you may see the ivy crawl.
The good man's ashes rest below;—
He's gone where all the righteous go.
I dug his grave with many a moan,
And almost wished it were my own.
I daily view the earthly bed,
Where Death has laid his reverend head;
And when I see a weed appear,
I pluck it up and shed a tear.
The parish grieved, for not an eye
In all its large extent was dry,
Save one:—but such a kindly grace
Ne'er decked the Lawyer's iron face.
The aged wept a friend long known,
The young a parent's loss bemoan:
While we, alas! shall long deplore
The bounteous patron of the poor."

The Doctor heard, with tearful eye,
The Sexton's grateful eulogy:
Then sought the stone with gentle tread,
As fearing to disturb the dead,
And thus, in measured tones, he read:

"For fifty years the Pastor trod
The way commanded by his God;
For fifty years his flock he fed
With that divine celestial bread
Which nourishes the better part,
And fortifies man's failing heart.
His wide, his hospitable door,
Was ever open to the poor;
While he was sought, for counsel sage,
By every rank and every age.
That counsel sage he always gave,
To warn, to strengthen, and to save:
He sought the sheep that went astray,
And pointed out the better way:
But while he with his smiles approved
The virtue he so dearly loved,
He did not spare the harsher part,
To probe the ulcer to the heart:
He sternly gave the wholesome pain
That brought it back to health again.
Thus, the commands of Heaven his guide,
He lived,—and then in peace he died."

SYNTAX.

"Pray tell me, friend, who now succeeds
This Pastor, famed for virtuous deeds?"

SEXTON.

"A very worthy, pious man,
Who does us all the good he can;
But he, good Sir, has got a wife;"

SYNTAX.

"Who may perhaps disturb his life,
A tongue sometimes engenders strife."

SEXTON.

"No:—she's a worthy woman too;
But then they've children not a few:
I think it is the will of Heaven
That they are bless'd with six or seven;
And then you will agree with me,
That home's the scene of charity."

SYNTAX.

"'Tis true;—nor can your Parson preach
A sounder doctrine than you teach.
And now, good Sexton, let me ask,
While you perform your mortal task,
As day and night you frequent tread
The dreary mansions of the dead,
If you, in very truth, can boast,
That you have ever seen a ghost?'

SEXTON.

"Your Reverence, no;—though some folks say
That such things have been seen as they.
Old women talk, in idle chat,
Of ghosts and goblins, and all that;

While, round the glimmering fire at night,
They fill their hearers with affright.
'Tis said that Doctor Worthy walks,
And up and down the church-yard stalks;
That often, when the moon shines bright,
His form appears all clad in white;
But to his soul it is not given
To walk on earth—for that's in Heaven.
All hours I have crossed this place,
And ne'er beheld a spirit's face.
Once, I remember, late at night,
I something saw, both large and white,
Which made me stop, and made me stare,—
But 'twas the Parson's grizzle mare.
Such things as these, I do believe,
The foolish people oft deceive;
And then the parish gossips talk
How witches dance, and spectres walk."

SYNTAX.

"Your reasoning I much commend;
So fare you well, my honest friend.
If we act right we need not dread
Either the living or the dead:
The spirit that disturbs our rest
Is a bad conscience in our breast;
With that a man is doubly curst:"

SEXTON.

"That spirit haunted Lawyer Thrust."

SYNTAX.

"His race is run, his work is o'er—
The wicked man can sin no more;

He's gone where justice will be done
To all who live beneath the sun:
And, though he wronged you when alive,
Let not your vengeance thus survive:
Forgive him, now he's laid so low—
Nor trample on a fallen foe.
Once more farewell! But ere we part,
There's something that will cheer your heart."

SEXTON.

"Your Reverence, 'twill be some time yet
Ere I forgive;—but to forget—
No, no, for though I may forgive,
I can't forget him while I live.
For your good gift, kind Heaven I bless,
And wish you health and happiness:
I thank my God, each coming day,
For what he gives and takes away:
And now I thank him, good and just,
That he has taken Lawyer Thrust."

Syntax along the village passed,
And to the Dragon came at last;
Where, as the shepherd-boy had said,
There seemed to be a busy trade:
And, seated in an easy chair,
He found that all he wished was there.

CANTO IX.

Along the varying road of Life,
In calm content, in toil or strife;
At morn or noon, by night or day,
As time conducts him on his way,
How oft doth man, by Care oppressed,
Find in an Inn a place of rest!
Whether, intent on worldly views,
He, in deep thought, his way pursues;
Whether, by airy pleasure led,
Or by Hope's fond delusions fed,
He bids adieu to home, and strays
Through unknown paths and distant ways;
Where'er his fancy bids him roam,
In every Inn he finds a home.
—Should Fortune change her favouring wind,
Though former friends should prove unkind,
Will not an Inn his cares beguile,
Where on each face he sees a smile?
When cold winds blow, and tempests lower,
And the rain pours in angry shower,
The dripping traveller looks around,
To see what shelter may be found:
Then on he drives, through thick and thin,
To the warm shelter of an Inn.
Whoe'er would turn their wandering feet,
Assured the kindest smiles to meet;

Whoe'er would go, and not depart
But with kind wishes from the heart,
O let them quit the world's loud din,
And seek the comforts of an Inn:
And as the Doric SHENSTONE sung,
With plaintive music on his tongue—
"Whoe'er has travelled Life's dull round,
  Where'er his changeful tour has been,
Will sigh to think how oft he found
  His warmest welcome at an Inn."

'Twas at an Inn, in calm repose,
Heedless of human joys or woes,
That Syntax passed a quiet night
In pleasing dreams and slumbers light;
But in the morn the thunder roared,
The clouds their streaming torrents poured;
The angry winds impetuous blew,
The rattling casement open flew.
Scared at the noise, he reared his head;
Then, starting quickly from the bed,
"Is it," he cried, "the day of doom?"
As he bestrode the trembling room.
The houses' tops with water streamed,
The village-street a river seemed:
While, at the tempest all amazed,
The rustics from their windows gazed,
"I'm not," he said, "disposed to fear,
But 'tis not time to loiter here;
I'll change the scene, and quick retire
From flaming flash to kitchen fire;

Nay, while rude Nature's threats prevail,
I'll lose the storm in toast and ale."
Half-dressed he made a quick retreat,
And in the kitchen took his seat,
Where an old woman told the host
What by the lightning she had lost;
How a blue flash her sow had struck,
Had killed a cock and lamed a duck!
With open mouth another came,
To tell a rick was in a flame;
And then declared that on the spire
He saw the weathercock on fire:
Nay, that so loud the winds were singing,
They'd set the peal of bells a-ringing!
A dripping tailor entered next
And preached upon the self-same text:
He swore, that, sitting on his board,
While the wind blew and thunder roared,
A kind of fiery flame came pop,
And bounced, and ran about his shop;
Now here, now there, so quick and nimble,
It singed his finger through his thimble;
That all about his needles ran,
If there was any truth in man;
While buttons, at least half-a-score,
Were driven through the kitchen door!
The Sexton, with important mien,
Gave his opinion on the scene;
And, to the Doctor drawing near,
Thus gently whispered in his ear:
"The Devil himself his cell has burst,
To fly away with Lawyer Thrust."

Now, having with due patience heard
The story which each wight preferred,
Syntax was to the parlour shown,
Where he might breakfast all alone.
"I see," said he, "I here must stay,
And at the Dragon pass the day:
And this same Dragon, on my life,
Just hints that I have got a wife;
Nor can I pass the morning better
Than to indite this wife a letter."
He paused and sighed ere he began,
When thus the fond epistle ran.

"My dearest Doll,—full many a day
From you and home I've been away;
But, though we thus are doomed to part,
You're ever present to my heart:
Whene'er my prayers to Heaven arise,
At morn or evening sacrifice,
Whene'er for Heaven's care they sue,
I ask it for my Dolly too.
My Journey, like Life's common road,
Has had its evils and its good;
But I've no reason to complain,
When pleasure has outweighed the pain.
With flattering Fortune in my view,
Glad I the toilsome way pursue;
For I've no fear to make a book,
In which the world will like to look;
Nor do I doubt 'twill prove a Mine
For my own comfort and for thine!

But should all fail, I've found a friend
In my old school-mate, DICKY BEND;
Who, kind and wealthy, will repay,
If hope should cheat me on the way,
My every loss I may sustain,
And ease ill-fortune of its pain:
He has engaged to glad our home,
With promise of much good to come.
Particulars of what I've seen,
What I have done—where I have been,
I shall reserve for my return,
When, as the crackling faggots burn,
I will in all domestic glory,
Smoke out my pipe, and tell my story:
But, be assured, I'm free from danger;
To the world's tricks I'm not a stranger:
Whatever risks I'm forced to run,
I shall take care of number *one;*
While you, at home, will keep in view
The self-same care of number *two.*
To my kind neighbours I commend
The wishes of their distant friend:
Within ten days, perhaps a week,
I shall YORK's famous city seek,
Where at the post, I hope to find
A line from Dolly, ever kind.
And, if you will the pleasure crown,
Tell me the prattle of our town;
Of all that's passing, and has passed,
Since your dear Hub beheld it last:
And know the truth which I impart,
The offspring of my honest heart,

That wheresoe'er I'm doomed to roam,
I still shall find that Home is Home:
That true to Love and nuptial vows,
I shall remain your loving spouse.
Such are the tender truths I tell;
Conjux carissima—farewell!"

Thus he his kindest thoughts revealed—
But scarce had he the letter sealed,
When straight appeared the trembling Host,
Looking as pale as any ghost:—
"A man's just come into the town,
Who says the castle's tumbled down:
And that, with one tremendous blow,
The lightning's force has laid it low."
"What castle, friend?" the Doctor cried.
"The castle by the river side;
A famous place, where, as folks say,
Some great king lived in former day:
But this fine building long has been
A sad and ruinated scene,
Where owls, and bats, and starlings dwell,—
And where, alas, as people tell,
At the dark hour when midnight reigns,
Ghosts walk, all armed, and rattle chains."
"Peace, peace," said Syntax, "peace, my friend,
Nor to such tales attention lend.
—But this new thought I must pursue:
A castle, and a ruin too;
I'll hasten there,—and take a view."

The storm was past and many a ray
Of Phœbus now revived the day,

When Grizzle to the door was brought,
And this famed spot the Doctor sought.
Upon a rock the castle stood,
Three sides environed by a flood,
Where confluent streams uniting lave
The craggy rift with foaming wave.
Around the moss-clad walls he walked,
Then through the inner chambers stalked;
And thus exclaimed with look profound,
The echoes giving back the sound.
"Let me expatiate here awhile:
I think this antiquated pile
Is, doubtless, in the Saxon style.
This was a noble, spacious hall,
But why the chapel made so small?
I fear our fathers took more care
Of festive hall than house of prayer.
I find these Barons fierce and bold,
Who proudly lived in days of old,
To prayer preferred a sumptuous treat,
Nor went to pray when they could eat.
Here all along the banners hung;
And here the welcome minstrels sung:
The walls with glittering arms bedight
Displayed an animating sight:
Beneath that arch-way, once a gate,
With helmed crest, in warlike state
The bands marched forth, nor feared the toil,
Of bloody war that gave the spoil.
But now, alas! no more remains
Than will reward the painter's pains:

The palace of the feudal victor
Now serves for nought but for a picture.
Plenty of water here I see,
But what's a view without a tree?
There's something grand in yonder tower,
But not a shrub to make a bower;
Howe'er, I'll try to take the view,
As well as my best art can do."

An heap of stones the Doctor found,
Which loosely lay upon the ground,
To form a seat, where he might trace
The antique beauty of the place:
But, while his eye observed the line
That was to limit the design,
The stones gave way, and sad to tell,
Down from the bank he headlong fell.
The slush collected for an age,
Received the venerable Sage;
For, at the time, the ebbing flood
Was just retreating from the mud:
So, after floundering about,
Syntax contrived to waddle out,
Half-stunned, amazed, and covered o'er
As seldom wight had been before.
O'erwhelmed with mud, and stink, and grief,
He saw no house to give relief;
So thus amid the village din,
He ran the gauntlet to the inn.
An angler threw his hook so pat,
He caught at once the Doctor's hat;

A bathing boy, who naked stood,
Dashed boldly in the eddying flood,
And, swimming onward like a grig,
Soon overtook the Doctor's wig.
Grizzle had traced the barren spot,
Where not a blade of grass was got:
And, finding nought to tempt her stay,
She to the Dragon took her way.
The ostler cried, "Here's some disaster—
The mare's returned without her master!"
But soon he came amid the noise
Of men and women, girls and boys:
Glad in the inn to find retreat
From the rude insult of the street.

Undressed, well washed, and put to bed,
With mind disturbed, and aching head,
In vain poor Syntax sought repose,
But lay and counted all his woes.
The friendly Host, with anxious care,
Now hastes the posset to prepare:—
The cordial draught he kindly gives;
Which Syntax with a smile receives:
Then seeks, in sleep, a pause from sorrow,
In hopes of better fate to-morrow.

CANTO X.

Poor mortal man, in every state,
What troubles and what ills await!
His transient joy is chased by sorrow,
To-day he's blest;—a wretch to-morrow.
When in the world he first appears,
He hails the light with cries and tears:
A school-boy next, he fears the nod
Of pedant power, and feels the rod:
When to an active stripling grown,
The Passions seize him as their own;
Now lead him here, now drive him there,
The alternate sport of Joy and Care;
Allure him with their glittering treasure,
Or give the brimming cup of pleasure;
While one eludes his eager haste,
The other palls upon the taste.
The pointed darts from Cupid's quiver,
Wound his warm heart and pierce his liver;
While charmed by fair Belinda's eyes,
He dines on groans and sups on sighs.
If from this gay and giddy round
He should escape both safe and sound,
Perhaps, if all things else miscarry,
He takes it in his head to marry;
And in this lottery of life,
If he should draw a scolding wife,

With a few children, eight or ten
(For such things happen now and then),
Poor hapless man! he knows not where
To look around without a care.
Ambition, in its airy flight,
May tempt him to some giddy height;
But, ere the point he can attain,
He tumbles ne'er to rise again.
Pale Avarice may his heart possess,
The bane of human happiness,
Which never feels for others' woe,
Nor ever does a smile bestow;
A wretched, meagre, griping elf,
A foe to all, and to himself.
Then comes Disease, with baneful train,
And the pale family of Pain:
Till Death appears in awful state,
And calls him to the realms of Fate.
—How oft is Virtue seen to feel
The woeful turn of Fortune's wheel,
While she with golden stores awaits,
The wicked in their very gates.
But Virtue still the value knows
Of honest deeds, and can repose
Upon the flint her naked head;
While Vice lies restless on the bed
Of softest down, and courts in vain
The opiate to relieve its pain.

It was not Vice that e'er could keep
Dear Syntax from refreshing sleep;

For no foul thought, no wicked art,
In his pure life e'er bore a part:
Some ailment dire his slumbers broke,
And ere the sun arose, he woke;
When such a tremor o'er him passed,
He thought that hour would prove his last.
His limbs were all besieged by pain;
He now grew hot, then cold again:
His tongue was parched, his lips were dry,
And, heaving the unbidden sigh,
He rang the bell, and called for aid,
And groaned so loud, the affrighted maid
Spread the alarm throughout the house;
When straight the landlord and his spouse
Made all dispatch to do their best
And ease the sufferings of their guest.
"Have you a Doctor?" Syntax said;
"If not, I shortly shall be dead."
"O yes; a very famous man;
He'll cure you, Sir, if physic can.
I'll fetch him quick;—a man renowned
For his great skill the country round."

The Landlord soon the Doctor brought,
Whose words were grave, whose looks were
thought:
By the bed-side he took his stand,
And felt the patient's burning hand;
Then, with a scientific face,
He told the symptoms of the case.
"His frame's assailed with feverish heats;
His pulse with rapid movement beats;

And now, I think, 'twould do him good,
Were he to lose a little blood:
Some other useful matters too,
To ease his pain, I have in view.
I'll just step home, and, in a trice,
Will bring the fruits of my advice;
In the mean time, his thirst assuage
With tea that's made of balm or sage."
He soon returned,—his skill applied,—
From the vein flowed the crimson tide:
And as the folk behind him stand,
He thus declared his stern command:
"At nine these powders let him take;
At ten this draught,—the phial shake;
And you'll remember, at eleven,
Three of these pills must then be given;
This course you'll carefully pursue,
And give, at twelve, the bolus too:
If he should wander, in a crack
Clap this broad blister on his back;
And after he has had the blister,
Within an hour apply the clyster.
I must be gone; at three or four
I shall return with something more."

Now Syntax and his feverish state
Became the subject of debate.
The mistress said she was afraid
No medicine would give him aid;
For she had heard the screech-owl scream,
And had besides a horrid dream.

Last night the candle burned so blue;
While from the fire a coffin flew;
And, as she sleepless lay in bed,
She heard a death-watch at her head.
The maid and ostler too declared
That noises strange they both had heard.
"Ay," cried the Sexton, "these portend
To the sick man a speedy end;
And, when that I have drank my liquor,
I'll e'en go straight and fetch the Vicar."

The Vicar came, a worthy man,
And, like a good Samaritan,
Approached in haste the stranger's bed,
Where Syntax lay with aching head;
And, without any fuss or pother,
He offered to his reverend brother
His purse, his house, and all the care
Which a kind heart could give him there.

Says Syntax, in a languid voice,
"You make my very soul rejoice;
For, if within this house I stay,
My flesh will soon be turned to clay:
For the good Doctor means to pop
Into my stomach all his shop.
I think, dear Sir, that I could eat,
And physic's but a nauseous treat:
If all that stuff's to be endured,
I shall be killed in being cured."
"O," said the Vicar, "never fear;
We'll leave the apparatus here.

Come, quit your bed—I pray you, come,—
My arm shall bear you to my home,
Where I and my dear mate will find
Med'cine more suited to your mind."

Syntax now rose, but feeble stood,
From want of food and loss of blood;
But still he ventured to repair
To the good Vicar's house and care;
And found a dinner pretty picking,
In pudding boiled and roasted chicken.
Again, 'twas honest Grizzle's fate
To take her way through church-yard
gate;
And, undisturbed, once more to riot
In the green feast of church-yard diet.
The Vicar was at Oxford bred,
And had much learning in his head;
But, what was far the better part,
He had much goodness in his heart:
The Vicar also had a wife
The pride and pleasure of his life;
A loving, kind and friendly creature,
As blest in virtue as in feature,
Who, without blisters, drugs, or pills,
Her patient cured of all his ills.
Three days he stayed a welcome guest,
And eat and drank of what was best:
When on the fourth, in health renewed,
His anxious journey he pursued.

In two days more before his eyes
The stately towers of York arise.

"But what," said he, "can all this mean?
What is yon crowded busy scene?
Ten thousand souls I do maintain,
Are scattered over yonder plain."
"Ay, more than that," a man replied,—
Who trotted briskly by his side,
"And if you choose, I'll be your guide:
For sure you will not pass this way,
And miss the pleasure of the day:
These are the races, to whose sport
Nobles and gentry all resort."
Thought Syntax, I'll just take a look;
'Twill give a subject to my book.
So on they went;—the highway friend
His services did oft commend.
"I will attend you to the course,
And tell the name of every horse;
But first we'll go and take a whet,
And then I'll teach you how to bet:
I'll name the horse that's doomed to win—
We'll take the knowing fellows in."
Just as he spoke, the sports began;
The jockeys whipped, the horses ran;
And, when the coursers reached the post,
The man screamed out—"Your horse has
lost:
I've had the luck—I've won the day,
And you have twenty pounds to pay."
Syntax looked wild—the man said,
"Zounds!
You know you betted twenty pounds;

So pay them down, or you'll fare worse,
For I will flog you off the course."
The Doctor raved, and disavowed
The bold assertion to the crowd.
What would have been his hapless fate,
In this most unexpected state,
May well be guessed. But, lo! a friend
Fortune was kind enough to send:
An honest 'Squire, who smoked the trick,
Appeared well armed with oaken stick.
And placing many a sturdy blow
Upon the shoulders of the foe,
"It is with all my soul I beat
This vile, this most notorious cheat,"
The 'Squire exclaimed; "and you, good
folk,
Who sometimes love a pleasant joke,
As I am partly tired of thumping,
Should treat the scoundrel with a pump-
ing."
The crowd with their commission pleased,
Rudely the trembling Blackleg seized.
Who, to their justice forced to yield,
Soon ran off dripping from the field.

Syntax his simple story told,—
The 'Squire, as kind as he was bold,
His full protection now affords,
And cheered him both with wine and
words.
"I love the Clergy from my heart,
And always take a Parson's part.

My father, Doctor, wore the gown—
A better man was never known:
But an old uncle, a poor elf,
Who to save riches, starved himself,
By his last will bequeathed me clear
At least two thousand pounds a year,
And saved me all the pains at college,
To pore o'er books and aim at knowledge:
Thus free from care, I live at ease;
Go where I will, do what I please;
Pursue my sports, enjoy my pleasure,
Nor envy Lords their splendid treasure.
I have an house at York beside,
Where you shall go and straight reside:
And every kindness shall be shown,
Both for my Dad's sake, and your own:
For know, good Sir, I'm never loth
To mark my friendship for the Cloth.
Hearty's my name, and you shall find
A welcome, Doctor, to your mind:
And I've a wife so blithe and gay,
Who ne'er says yes when I say nay."
Syntax observed, "That was a blessing
A man might boast of in possessing."

At length arrived, a lady fair
Received them with a winning air.
"Ah," said the 'Squire, "I always come,
My dearest girl, with pleasure home:
You see a reverend Doctor here,
So give him of your choicest cheer:"
"Yes," she replied, "O yes, my dear."

7

"Nor fail all kindness to bestow:"
"O no, my dear," she said, "O no."
Thus happy Syntax joined the party
Of Madam and of 'Squire Hearty.

CANTO XI.

In this sad, variegated life,
Evil and good, in daily strife,
Contend, we find, which shall be master:
Now Fortune smiles—then sad disaster
Assumes in turn, its frowning power,
And gives to man his checkered hour.
With checkered hours good Syntax
thought,
And well he might, his journey fraught,
But still he hoped, when all was past,
That he should comfort find at last.
Thus, with unlooked-for kindness blest,
No fears alarm his tranquil breast;
He eats, and drinks, and goes to rest:
And when the welcome 'morrow came,
The 'Squire and Madam were the same.
Just as the Minster-clock struck nine,
Coffee and tea, and fowl and chine,
Appeared in all their due array,
To give the breakfast of the day.
The 'Squire then the talk began,
And thus the conversation ran.

'SQUIRE HEARTY.

"Doctor, you truly may believe
The pleasure which I now receive

In seeing you, as you sit there,
On what was once my father's chair.
I pray you think this house your home,—
Ay, though it were three months to come.
Here you will find yourself at ease—
May read or write—just as you please.
At nine we breakfast as you see,—
Dinner is always here at three;
At six my wife will give you tea."

MRS. HEARTY.

"And should you find the evening long,
I'll play a tune and sing a song."

'SQUIRE HEARTY.

"Besides, you'll range the country round;
Some curious things may there be found:
Your genius too may chance to trace,
Within this celebrated place,
Some ancient building worth a look,
That may, perhaps, enrich your book.
I'm a true Briton, as you see:
I love good cheer, and liberty;
And what I love myself, I'll give
To others, while I'm doomed to live.
This morning I intend to go
To see the military show.
The light dragoons now quartered here,
Will all in grand review appear:
They are a regiment of renown,
And some great General is come down
To see them all, in bright array,
Act the fierce battle of the day.

If you should like such sights as these:
If warlike feats your fancy please,
We'll to the Common take a ride,
And I myself will be your guide:
So, if you please, within an hour
Our nags shall be before the door."

SYNTAX.

"I will be ready to attend
The summons of my worthy friend.
The laurelled Hero's my delight,
With plumed crest and helmet bright:
E'en when a boy, at early age,
I read in Homer's lofty page
How the stout Greeks, in time of yore,
Brought havoc to the Phrygian shore:
I revelled in that ancient story,
And burned with ardent love of glory.
Whene'er I traced the fields of Troy,
My heart beat high with martial joy:
'Tis true, I pray that war may cease,
And Europe hail returning Peace;
Yet still I feel my bosom glow
When British heroes meet the foe;
When our armed legions make him fly,
And yield the palm of Victory:
Or when our naval thunders roar,
And terrify the Gallic shore.
This grand review will give me pleasure,
And I shall wait upon your leisure."

But, as no time was to be lost,
Syntax now hastened to the post:

The post obeyed his loud command,
And gave a letter to his hand.
With eager haste the seal he broke,
And thus the fond epistle spoke.

"My dearest husband,—on my life
I thought you had forgot your wife:
While she to her affection true,
Was always thinking, Love, on you.
By this time, I presume, you've made
No small advancement in your trade:
I mean, my dear, that this same book,
To which I with impatience look,
Is full of promise: and I'm bold
To hope for a return in gold.
I have no doubt that ample gains
Will well reward your learned pains,
And will with bounteous store, repay
Your anxious toil of many a day;
For well, my dearest friend, I know
Where'er you are compelled to go,
You still must sigh that you should be
So long away from Love and me.
I truly say my heart doth burn
With ardent wish for your return:
And that I may my Syntax greet
With all due honour when we meet,
The milliner is now preparing
A dress that will be worth the wearing;
Just such an one as I have seen
In Ackermann's last Magazine,

Where by the skilful painter's aid,
Each fashion is so well displayed.
A robe of crape with satin boddice,
Will make me look like any goddess:
A mantle too is all the ton,
And therefore I have ordered one:
I've also got a lilac bonnet,
And placed a yellow feather on it:
Thus I shall be so very smart,
'Twill vex Miss Raisin to the heart;
Oh! it will make me burst with laughter,
To plague the purse-proud grocer's daughter;
While through the town as you shall see
No one will be so fine as me.
Oh! with what pleasure and delight
I shall present me to your sight;
How shall I hug you, dearest honey,
When you return brimful of money."

Syntax exclaimed, in accents sad,
"The woman's surely gone stark mad!
To ruin, all her airs will tend;
But I'll read on, and see the end."

"As to the news, why you must know,
Things in their usual order go:
Jobson the Tanner's run away,
And has not left a doit to pay:
Bet Bumkin was last Thursday married,
And Mrs. Stillborn has miscarried.
In the High-street, the other day,
Good Mrs. Squeamish swooned away,

And was so ill, as it was said,
That she was borne away for dead;
But Mother Gossip, who knows all
The neighbours round, both great and small,
Has hinted to me, as she thinks,
That pious Mrs. Squeamish drinks.
—There is a Lady just come down,
A dashing, frisky dame from town,
To visit Madam Stapleton;
She's said to be a London toast,
But has no mighty charms to boast:
For it is clear to my keen sight,
That she lays on both red and white.
She drives about in chaise and pair,
And, I have heard, can curse and swear:
But I mind not these things, not I,
I never deal in calumny.
So fare you well, my dearest life,—
And I remain your loving wife."

POSTSCRIPT.

"But if you fear that you shall come
Without a bag of money home,
'Twere better far that you should take
A leap at once into the Lake:
I'd rather hear that you were drowned,
Than that you should my hopes confound."

These tender lines did not impart
Much comfort to the Doctor's heart;
He therefore thought it would be better
To lay aside this pretty letter;

Nor suffer its contents to sour
The pleasure of the present hour.

The 'Squire now became his guide,
So off they trotted, side by side;
And, ere they passed a mile or two,
Beheld the scene of the review.
The troops drawn up in proud array,
An animating sight display;
The well-formed squadrons wheel around;
The standards wave, the trumpets sound;
When Grizzle, long inured to war,
And not without an honoured scar,
Found all her former spirits glow
As when she used to meet the foe:
No ears she pricked, for she had none:
Nor cocked her tail, for that was gone:
But still she snorted, foamed, and flounced;
Then up she reared and off she bounced;
And, having played these pretty pranks,
Dashed all at once into the ranks;
While Syntax, though unused to fear,
Suspected that his end was near.
But, though his courage 'gan to addle,
He still stuck close upon his saddle;
While to the trumpets on the hill,
Grizzle sped fast, and then stood still:
With them she closed her warlike race,
And took with pride her ancient place;
For Grizzle, as we've told before,
Once to the wars a trumpet bore.

At length, recovered from his fright,
The Doctor stayed and viewed the sight;
And then, with heart as light as cork,
He with his friend jogged back to York,
Where was renewed the friendly fare,
And every comfort promised there.
The time in chit-chat passed away,
Till the chimes told the closing day:
"And now," says pleasant Madam Hearty,
"What think you if our little party
Should each to sing a song agree?
'Twill give a sweet variety.
Thus let the passing moments roll,
Till Thomas brings the evening bowl;
The Doctor, sure, will do his best
And kindly grant my poor request."
The Doctor, though by nature grave,
And rather formed to tune a stave,
Whene'er he got a little mellow,
Was a most merry pleasant fellow;
Would sing a song, or tell a riddle,
Or play a hornpipe on the fiddle;
And, being now a little gay,
Declared his wishes to obey.
"Then I'll begin," 'Squire Hearty said,
"But though by land my tours are made,
Whene'er I tune a song, or glee,
I quit the land, and go to sea."

THE 'SQUIRE'S SONG.

The signal given, we seek the main,
 Where tempests rage, and billows roar,
Nor know we if we e'er again
 Shall anchor on our native shore.

But, as through surging waves we sail,
 And distant seas and isles explore,
Hope whispers that some future gale
 Will waft us to our native shore.

When battle rages all amain,
 And hostile arms their vengeance pour,
We British sailors will maintain
 The honour of our native shore.

But, should we find a watery grave,
 A nation will our loss deplore;
And tears will mingle with the wave
 That breaks upon our native shore.

And after many a battle won,
 When every toil and danger's o'er,
How great the joy, each duty done,
 To anchor on our native shore!

MRS. HEARTY'S SONG.

Cupid, away! thy work is o'er:
 Go seek Idalia's flowery grove!
Your pointed darts will pain no more;
 Hymen has healed the wounds of Love.

Hymen is here, and all is rest;
 To distant flight thy pinions move:

No anxious doubts, no fears molest;
  Hymen has soothed the pangs of Love.

Cupid, away! the deed is done!
  Away, 'mid other scenes to rove:
For Ralph and Isabel are one,
  And Hymen guards the home of Love.

The Doctor now his reverence made,
And Madam's smiling nod obeyed.
"Your songs," said he, "have given me pleasure,
As well in subject as in measure;
But, in some modern songs, the taste
Is far, I'm sure, from being chaste:
They do not make the least pretence
To poetry or common sense.
Some coarse conceits, a lively air,
With a *da capo*, here and there,
Of uncouth words, which ne'er were found
In any language above ground:
And these set off with some strange phrase,
Compose our sing-song now-a-days.
The dancing-master of my school
In this way oft will play the fool,
And make one laugh—one knows not why,—
But we had better laugh than cry.
The song, which you're about to hear,
Will of this character appear;
From London it was sent him down,
As a great favourite through the town."

DOCTOR SYNTAX'S SONG.

I've got a scold of a wife,
The plague and storm of my life;
O! were she in coal-pit bottom,
And all such jades, 'od rot 'em!
My cares would then be over,
And I should live in clover;
With harum scarum, horum scorum,—
Stewed prunes for ever!
Stewed prunes for ever!

Brother Tom's in the codlin-tree,
As blithe as blithe can be:
While Dorothy sits below,
Where the daffodillies grow:
And many a slender rush,
And blackberries all on a bush;
With harum scarum, &c. &c.

We'll to the castle go
Like grenadiers all of a row,
While the horn and trump shall sound
As we pace the ramparts round,
Where many a lady fair
Comes forth to take the air,
With harum scarum, &c. &c.

The vessel spreads her sails
To catch the rising gales,
And dances o'er the wave;
While many a love-lorn slave

To his mistress tells his tale,
Far off in the distant vale;
With harum scarum, &c. &c.

When the dew is on the rose,
And the wanton zephyr blows;
When lilies raise their head,
And harebells fragrance shed,
Then I to the rocks will hie,
And sing a lullaby;
With harum scarum, &c. &c.

By famed Ilissus stream
How oft I fondly dream,
When I read in classic pages
Of all the ancient sages;
But they were born to die!
And so were you and I;
With harum scarum, horum scorum,
Stewed prunes for ever!
Stewed prunes for ever!

Thus, with many a pleasant lay,
The party closed the exhausted day.

CANTO XII.

Life is a journey,—on we go
Through many a scene of joy and woe:
Time flits along and will not stay,
Nor let us linger on the way:
Like as a stream, whose varying course
Now rushes with impetuous force;
Now in successive eddies plays,
Or in meanders gently strays,
It still moves on, till spreading wide,
It mingles with the briny tide;
And, when it meets the ocean's roar,
The limpid waves are seen no more.
Such, such is Life's uncertain way;—
Now the sun wakes the enlivening day:
The scene around enchants the sight;
To cool retreat the shades invite;
The blossoms balmy fragrance shed;
The meads a verdant carpet spread;
While the clear rill reflects below
The flowers that on its margin grow,
And the sweet songsters of the grove
Attune to harmony and love.
But lo! the clouds obscure the sky,
And tell the bursting tempest nigh:
The vivid flash, the pelting storm,
Fair Nature's every grace deform;

While their assailing powers annoy
The pensive pilgrim's tranquil joy:
But, though no tempests should molest
The bower where he stops to rest,
Care will not let him long remain,
But sets him on his way again.
Thus Syntax, whom the 'Squire had pressed
For three whole months to take his rest,
Sighed when he found he could not stay
To loiter through another day:
"No," he exclaimed, "I must away:—
I have a splendid book to make,
To form a Tour,—to paint a Lake:
And, by a well-projected Tome,
To carry fame and money home:
And, should I fail, my loving wife
Will lead me such a precious life,
That I had better never more
Approach my then forbidden door."
'Twas thus he pondered as he lay,
When the sun told another day,
Nor long the downy couch he pressed,
Where busy thought disturbed his rest:
But quick prepared, with grateful heart,
From this warm mansion to depart.
The 'Squire to his professions true,
Thus spoke at once his kind adieu.

'SQUIRE.

"I'm sorry, Sir, with all my heart,
That you and I so soon must part:

Your virtues my regard engage;
I venerate the reverend sage;
And, though I've not the mind to toil
In Learning's way, by midnight oil,
Yet still I feel the reverence due
To all such learned men as you:
Nor can I urge your longer stay,
When Science calls you far away:
But still I hope you'll not refuse
My friendly tribute to the Muse;
And, when again you this way come,
Again you'll find this house a home.
Besides, I mean to recommend
Your labours to a noble friend,
Who well is known to rank as high
In learning, as in quality;
Who can your merits well review;
A statesman, and a poet too:
He will your genius truly scan,
And though a Lord, a learned man.
For C****** is an honoured name,
Whose virtue and unsullied fame
Will decorate the historic page,
And live through every future age.
That courteous Lord doth condescend
To know me for a faithful friend;
And, when you to his Lordship give
The letter which you now receive,
Expect, on his right noble part,
A welcome that will cheer your heart.
To —— ——— then repair,
And Honour will attend you there.

Nor fear, my friend, that gilded state
Will frown upon your humble fate;
My Lord is good as he is great."

SYNTAX.

"Your kindness, surely, knows no end;
You are in truth a real friend;
Nor can my feeble tongue express
This unexpected happiness:
For if this noble Lord should deign
My feeble labours to sustain,
With the all-cheering, splendid rays
Of his benign, protecting praise,
My fortune will at once be made,
And I shall bless the author's trade."

Thus as he spoke, 'Squire Hearty gave
The letter Syntax longed to have;
And with it a soft silky note,
On which two coal-black words were wrote;
The sight of which his sense confounds,
For these said words were Twenty Pounds.
"Check," said the 'Squire, "your won-
dering look;
'Tis my subscription to your book;
And when 'tis printed, you will send
A copy to your Yorkshire friend;
Besides, I'll try to sell a score
Among my neighbours here, or more."

The Doctor's tongue made no reply,
But his heart heaved a grateful sigh:

Nor, as he sits, can we do better
Than to repeat the promised letter.

"My Lord,
This liberty I take,
For Laughter and for Merit's sake;
And when the bearer shall appear
In your fine mansion's atmosphere,
His figure will your spirits cheer.
You need no other topic seek;
He'll furnish laughter for a week:
But still I say, and tell you true,
You'll love him for his merit too.
You'll see, at once, in this Divine,
Quixote and Parson Adams shine:
An hero well combined you'll view
For Fielding and Cervantes too:
Besides, my Lord, if I can judge,
In classic lore he's used to drudge.
O do but hear his simple story;
Let him but lay it all before you;
And you will thank me for my letter,
And say that you are Hearty's debtor:
Nay, when your sides are tired with mirth,
Your heart will feel his real worth.
I know your kindness will receive him,
And to your favour thus I leave him.
So I remain, with zeal most fervent,
Your Lordship's true and hearty servant.
York, Thursday. R. H."

The Doctor now prepared to go,
With heart of joy and look of woe;
He silent squeezed the 'Squire's hands,
And asked of Madam her commands.
The 'Squire exclaimed, "Why so remiss?
She bids you take a hearty kiss;
And if you think that one won't do,
I beg, dear Sir, you'll give her *two.*"
"Nay, then," says Syntax, "you shall see;"
And straight he gave the Lady *three;*
Nor did he linger to exclaim,
"He ne'er had kissed a fairer dame."
The Lady blushing thanked him too,
And in soft accents said—"Adieu."

Syntax, since first he left his home,
Had no such view of good to come,
As now before his fancy rose
To bid him laugh at future woes.
"Fortune," he cried, "is kind at last,
And I forgive her malice past:
Clad in C———'s benignant form,
Her power no more will wake the storm,
Nor e'er again her anger shed
In frequent showers upon my head."

Now, after a short morning's ride,
In eager Hope and Fancy's pride,
The Doctor views, with conscious smile,
Fair ——— ————'s splendid pile.
Not Versailles makes a finer show,
As, passing o'er the lofty brow,
The stately scene is viewed below.

My Lord received him with a grace
Which marked the sovereign of the place;
Nor was poor Syntax made to feel
The pride which fools so oft reveal;
Who think it a fine state decorum,
When humble merit stands before 'em:
But here was birth from folly free;
Here was the true nobility,
Where human kindness gilds the crest—
The first of virtues, and the best.

An hour in pleasant chit-chat past,
The welcome dinner came at last:
And now the hungry Syntax eats
Of high ragouts and dainty meats:
Nor was the good man found to shrink
Whenever he was asked to drink.

MY LORD.

"What think you, Doctor, of the show
Of pictures that around you glow?"

SYNTAX.

"I'll by-and-by enjoy the treat:
But now, my Lord, I'd rather eat."

MY LORD.

"What say you to this statue here?
—Does it not flesh and blood appear?"

SYNTAX.

"I'm sure, my Lord, 'tis very fine;
But I, just now, prefer your wine."

SIR JOHN.

"I wonder you can keep your eye
From forms that do with Nature vie;
Nay, in my mind, my reverend friend,
Nature's best works they far transcend.
Look at that picture of the Graces,
What lovely forms!—what charming faces!"

SYNTAX.

"Their charms, Sir John, I shall discover,
I have no doubt, when dinner's over:
At present, if to judge I'm able,
The finest works are on the table.
I should prefer the cook just now,
To Rubens or to Gerrard Dow."

MY LORD.

"I wish to judge, by certain rules,
The Flemish and Italian schools;
And nicely to describe the merits
Or beauties which each school inherits."

SYNTAX.

"Though in their way they're both be-
witching,
I now prefer vour Lordship's kitchen."

The dinner done, the punch appears,
And many a glass their spirits cheers,
The festive hours thus passed away,
Till time brought on the closing day:
The Doctor talked, nor ceased his quaffing,
While all around were sick with laughing.

MY LORD.

"Again the subject I renew,
And wish you would the pictures view."

SYNTAX.

"To view them now would be a trouble,
For faith, my Lord, my eyes see double."

MY LORD.

"To bed, then, we had best repair,—
I give you to the Butler's care;
A sage grave man, who will obey
Whate'er your Reverence has to say."

The sage grave man appeared, and bowed:
"I am of this good office proud;
But 'tis the custom of this place,
From country yeoman to his Grace,
Whene'er a stranger guest we see,
To make him of the cellar free.
To you the same respect we bear,
And therefore beg to lead you there;
Where every noble butt doth claim
The honour of some titled name."

The servants waited on the stairs,
With cautious form and humble airs.
"Lead on," says Syntax, "I'll not stay,
But follow where you lead the way."

The Butler cried, "You'll understand
It is our noble Lord's command

To give this reverend Doctor here
A sample of our strongest beer;
So tap her Grace of Devonshire."

At length the potent liquor flows,
Which makes poor man forget his woes.
Syntax exclaimed, "Here's Honour's boast;—
The health of our most noble Host—
And let fair Devon crown the toast.'

The cups were cheered with loyal song;
But cups like these ne'er lasted long:
And Syntax stammered, "Do you see?
Now I'm of this famed cellar free,
I wish I might be quickly led
To enjoy my freedom in a bed."
He wished but once, and was obeyed,
And soon within a bed was laid,
Where, all the day's strange business o'er,
He now was left to sleep and snore.

CANTO XIII.

How oft, as through Life's vale we stray,
Doth Fancy light us on our way!
How oft, with many a vision bright,
Doth she the wayward heart delight,
And, with a fond enlivening smile,
The heavy hour of care beguile!
But though so oft she scatters flowers,
To make more gay our waking hours,
Night is the time when o'er the soul
She exercises full control.
While Life's more active functions pause,
And sleep its sable curtain draws,
'Tis then she waves her fairy wand:
And strange things rise at her command:
She then assumes a motley reign,
And man lives o'er his life again;
While many an airy dream invites
Her wizard masks, her wanton sprites:
Through the warm brain the phantoms play,
And form a visionary day.

Thus Syntax, while the bed he pressed,
And passed the night in balmy rest,
Was led in those unconscious hours,
By Fancy, to her fairy bowers,

Where the light spirits wander free
In whimsical variety.

No more an humble Curate now,
He feels a mitre on his brow;
The mildewed surplice, thus withdrawn,
Yields to the fine, transparent lawn;
And peruke, that defied all weather,
Is nicely dressed to ape a feather.
Grizzle no more is seen to wail
Her mangled ears and butchered tail:
Six Grizzles now, with every ear,
And all their flowing tails appear;
When harnessed to a light barouche,
The ground they do not seem to touch;
While onward whirled in wild surprise,
The air-blown Prelate thinks he flies.
Now through the long cathedral aisle,
Where vergers bow and virgins smile,
With measured step and solemn air,
He gains at length the sacred chair;
And to the crowd, with look profound,
Bestows his holy blessing round.
Above the pealing organs blow,
To the respondent choir below;
When, bending to religion's shrine,
He feels an energy divine.
Now, 'scaped from Dolly's angry clutches,
He thinks he's married to a Duchess,
And that her rank and glowing beauty
Enliven his prelatic duty.

Thus Fancy, with her antic train,
Passed nimbly through the Doctor's brain:
But while she told her varying story
Of short-lived pomp and fading glory,
A voice upon the vision broke,—
When Syntax gave a grunt—and 'woke.

"And may it please you, I've a word
To tell your Reverence, from my Lord."
"A Lord," he cried, "why, to be free,
I've been as good a Lord as he:
Throughout the night, I've been as great
As any Lord, with all his state;
But now that fine-drawn scene is o'er,
And I'm poor Syntax as before.
You spoiled my fortune, 'tis most certain,
The moment you withdrew the curtain:
So, if you please, my pretty maid,
You'll tell me what my Lord has said."
"—My Lord has sent to let you know
That breakfast is prepared below."
"—Let my respects upon him wait,
And say that I'll be with him straight."
Out then he bounced upon the floor:
The maid ran shouting through the door,
So much the figure of the Doctor,
In his unrobed condition shocked her.

Syntax now hastened to obey
The early summons of the day.
He humbly bowed and took his seat;
Nor did his Lordship fail to greet

With kindest words his reverend guest—
As how he had enjoyed his rest;
Hoped every comfort he had found;
That his night's slumbers had been sound;
And that he was prepared to share
With keen regard, his morning's fare.
The Doctor smiled, and soon made free
With my Lord's hospitality;
Then told aloud his golden dream,
Which proved of mirth a fruitful theme.
"'Tis true," he said, "when I awoke,
The charm dissolved, the spell was broke;
The mitre and its grand display,
With my fine wife, all passed away:
The awakening voice my fortune crossed:
I oped my eyes, and all was lost;—
But still I find, to my delight,
I have not lost my appetite."

SIR JOHN.

"As for the mitre and the gold,
Which Fancy gave you to behold,
They, to a mind with learning fraught,
Do not deserve a passing thought:
But I lament that such a bride
Should thus be stolen from your side."

SYNTAX.

"For that choice good I need not roam;
I've got, Sir John, a wife at home,
Who can from morn to night contrive
To keep her family alive:

Such sprightly measures she can take
That no one sleeps when she's awake.
For me, if Fortune would but shower
Some portion of her wealth and power,
I would forgive her, on my life,
Though she forgot to add a wife.
Indeed, Sir John, we don't agree
Nor join in our philosophy;
For did you know what that man knows,
Had you e'er felt his cutting woes,
Who has of taunts a daily plenty,
Whose head is combed, whose pocket's
empty;
You ne'er would call those shiners trash,
Whose touch is life—whose name is Cash."

MY LORD.

"A truce, I pray, to your debate;
The hunters all impatient wait;
And much I hope our learned Clerk
Will take a gallop in the Park."

SYNTAX.

"Your sport, my Lord, I cannot take,
For I must go and hunt a Lake;
And while you chase the flying deer,
I must fly off to Windermere.
'Stead of hallooing to a fox,
I must catch echoes from the rocks;
With curious eye and active scent,
I on the picturesque am bent;
This is my game, I must pursue it,
And make it where I cannot view it:

Though in good truth, but do not flout me,
I bear that self-same thing about me.
If in man's form you wish to see
The picturesque, pray look at me;
I am myself without a flaw,
The very picturesque I draw.
A Rector, on whose face so sleek
In vain you for a wrinkle seek;
In whose fair form, so fat and round,
No obtuse angle's to be found;
On such a shape no man of taste
Would his fine tints or canvas waste:
But take a Curate who's so thin,
His bones seem peeping through his skin:
Make him to stand, or walk or sit,
In any posture you think fit,
And, with all these nice points about him,
No well-taught painter e'er would scout him:
For with his air, and look and mien,
He'd give effect to any scene.
In my poor beast, as well as me,
A fine example you may see:
She's so abrupt in all her parts—
O what fine subjects for the arts!
Thus, thus we travel on together,
With gentle gale or stormy weather:
And, though we trot along the plains,
Where one dead level ever reigns,
Or pace where rocks and mountains rise,
Who lift their heads, and brave the skies;

I Doctor Syntax, and my horse,
Give to the landscape double force.
—I have no doubt I shall produce
A volume of uncommon use,
That will be worthy to be placed
Beneath the eye of men of taste;
And I should hope, my Lord, that you
Will praise it and protect it too;
Will let your all-sufficient name
The two-fold patronage proclaim:
That time may know, till time doth end,
That C——— was my honoured friend."

SIR JOHN.

"And can you, learned Doctor, see
When that important hour shall be?"

SYNTAX.

"Sir Knight, that was not wisely spoke;
The point's too serious for a joke;
And you must know, by Heaven's decree,
That hour will come to you and me,
And then succeeds—Eternity."

MY LORD.

"Peace, peace, Sir John, and let me tell
The Doctor that I wish him well.
I doubt not but his work will prove
Most useful to the arts I love.
But pray, good Sir, come up to town,
The seat of wealth and of renown:
Come up to town nor fear the cost,
Nor time nor labour shall be lost.

I'll ope my door and take you in—
You've made me laugh, and you shall win:
We'll then consult how I can best
Advance your real interest:
And here this piece of writing take;
You'll use it for the donor's sake;
I mean, you see, that it shall crown
Your wishes while you stay in town:
But you may, as it suits you, use it,
No one, I fancy, will refuse it."
The Doctor, when he viewed the paper,
Instead of bowing—cut a caper.

My Lord now sought the expected chase,
And Syntax in his usual pace,
When four long tedious days had past,
The town of Keswick reached at last,
Where he his famous work prepared,
Of all his toil the hoped reward.

Soon as the morn began to break,
Old Grizzle bore him to the Lake.
Along the banks he gravely paced,
And all its various beauties traced;
When, lo, a threatening storm appeared!
Phœbus the scene no longer cheered;
The dark clouds sunk on every hill:
The floating mists the valleys fill:
Nature, transformed, began to lour,
And threatened a tremendous shower.
"I love," he cried, "to hear the rattle.
When elements contend in battle;

For I insist, though some may flout it,
Who write about it, and about it,
That we the picturesque may find
In thunder loud, or whistling wind:
And often, as I fully ween,
It may be heard as well as seen:
For, though a pencil cannot trace
A sound as it can paint a place,
The pen, in its poetic rage,
Can make it figure on the page."

A fisherman, who passed that way,
Thought it civility to say—
"An' please you, Sir, 'tis all in vain
To take your prospects in the rain;
On horseback too you'll ne'er be able—
'Twere better sure to get a table."—
"Thanks," Syntax said, "for your advice,
And faith I'll take it in a trice;
For, as I'm moistened to the skin,
I'll seek a table at the Inn;"—
But Grizzle, in her haste to pass,
Lured by a tempting tuft of grass,
A luckless step now chanced to take,
And soused the Doctor in the Lake;
But, as it proved, no worse disaster
Befell poor Grizzle and her master,
Than both of them could well endure,
And a warm Inn would shortly cure.
To that warm Inn they quickly hied,
Where Syntax, by the fire-side,

9

Sat in the Landlord's garments clad,
But neither sorrowful nor sad;
Nor did hc waste his hours away,
But gave his pencil all its play,
And traced the landscapes of the day.

CANTO XIV.

"NATURE, dear Nature, is my goddess,
Whether arrayed in rustic boddice,
Or when the nicest touch of Art
Doth to her charms new charms impart:
But still I, somehow, love her best,
When she's in ruder mantle dressed:
I do not mean in shape grotesque,
But when she's truly picturesque."

Thus the next morning as he strayed,
And the surrounding scene surveyed,
Syntax exclaimed.—A party stood
Just on the margin of the flood,
Who were, in *statu quo*, to make
A little voyage on the Lake.
The Doctor forward stepped to show
The wealth of his port-folio:
The ladies were quite pleased to view
Such pretty pictures as he drew;
While a young man, a neighbouring 'Squire,
Expressed a very warm desire,
Which seemed to come from honest heart,
That of their boat he'd take a part.

Now from the shore they quickly sailed;
And soon the Doctor's voice prevailed.

"This is a lovely scene of nature:
But I've enough of land and water:
I want some living thing to show
How far the picturesque will go."

LADY.

"See, Sir, how swift the swallows fly;
And lo, the lark ascends on high;
We scarce can view him in the sky.
Behold the wild-fowl, how they spread
Upon the Lake's expansive bed:
The kite sails through the airy way,
Prepared to pounce upon its prey:
The rooks too, from their morning food,
Pass cawing to the distant wood."

SYNTAX.

"When with a philosophic eye
The realms of Nature I descry,
And view the grace that she can give
To all the varying forms that live;
I feel with awe the plastic art
That doth such wondrous powers impart
To all that wing the air, or creep
Along the earth, or swim the deep.
I love the winged world that flies
Through the thin azure of the skies;
Or, not ordained those heights to scan,
Live the familiar friends of man,
And, in his yard or round his cot,
Enjoy, poor things! their destined lot;
But though their plumes are gay with dyes,
In endless bright diversities,

What though such glowing tints prevail,
When the proud peacock spreads his tail;
What though the nightingales prolong
Through the charmed night the enchanting
 song;
What though the blackbird and the thrush
Make vocal every verdant bush;
Not one among the winged kind
Presents an object to my mind:
Their grace and beauty's nought to me;
In all their vast variety
The picturesque I cannot see.
A carrion fowl tied to a stake
Will a far better picture make,
When as a scare-crow 'tis displayed
To make all thievish birds afraid,
Than the white swan, in all its pride,
Sailing upon the crystal tide.
As a philosopher I scan
Whate'er kind Heaven has made for man;
I feel it a religious duty
To bless its use and praise its beauty:
I care not whatsoe'er the creature,
Whate'er its name, its form and feature,
So that fond Nature will aver
The creature doth belong to her.
But though indeed, I may admire
The greyhound's form and snake's attire,
They neither will my object suit
Like a good shaggy, ragged brute.
I will acknowledge that a goose
Is a fine fowl of sovereign use:

But for a picture she's not fitted—
The bird was made but to be spitted.
The pigeon, I'll be bound to show it,
Is a fine subject for a poet;
In the soft verse his mate he woos,
Turns his gay neck, and bills and coos,
And, as in amorous strut he moves,
Soothes the fond heart of him who loves:
But I'll not paint him, no, not I—
I like him better in a pie,
Well rubbed with salt and spicy dust,
And thus embodied in a crust.
How many a bird that haunts the wood,
How many a fowl that cleaves the flood,
With their sweet songs enchant my ear,
Or please my eye as they appear,
When in their flight, or as they row,
Delighted on the lake below!
But still, whate'er their form or feather,
You cannot make them group together;
For let them swim or let them fly,
The picturesque they all defy.
The bird that's sitting quite alone
Is fit but to be carved in stone;
And any man of taste 'twould shock
To paint those wild geese in a flock:
Though I like not a single figure,
Whether 'tis lesser or 'tis bigger:
That fisherman so lean and lank,
Who sits alone upon the bank,
Tempts not the eye; but, doff his coat,
And quickly group him with a boat,

You then will see the fellow make
A pretty object on the Lake.
If a boy's playing with a hoop,
'Tis something, for it forms a group.
In painter's eyes—O what a joke
To place a bird upon an oak:
At the same time, 'twould help the jest,
Upon the branch to fix a nest.
A trout, with all its pretty dyes
Of various hues, delights the eyes;
But still it is a silly whim
To make him on a canvas swim:
Yet, I must own, that dainty fish
Looks very handsome in a dish!
And he must be a thankless sinner
Who thinks a trout a paltry dinner.

"The first, the middle, and the last,
In picturesque is bold contrast;
And painting has no nobler use
Than this grand object to produce.
Such is my thought, and I'll pursue it;
There's an example—you shall view it.
Look at that tree—then take a glance
At its fine, bold protuberance;
Behold those branches—how their shade
Is by the mass of light displayed:
Look at that light, and see how fine
The backward shadows make it shine:
The sombre clouds that spot the sky,
Make the blue vaulting twice as high;

And where the sun-beams warmly glow,
They make the hollow twice as low.
The Flemish painters all surpass
In making pictures smooth as glass:
In Cuyp's best works there's pretty
painting:
But the bold picturesque is wanting.

"Thus, though I leave the birds to sing,
Or cleave the air with rapid wing—
Thus, though I leave the fish to play
Till the net drags them into day—
Kind Nature, ever bounteous mother!
Contrives it in some way or other,
Our proper wishes to supply
In infinite variety.
The world of quadrupeds displays
The painter's art in various ways;
But, 'tis some shaggy, ragged brute
That will my busy purpose suit;
Or such as, from their shape and make,
No fine wrought, high-bred semblance
take.
A well-fed horse, with shining skin,
Formed for the course, and plates to win,
May have his beauties, but not those
That will my graphic art disclose:
My raw-boned mare is worth a score
Of those fine pampered beasts, and more,
To give effect to bold design,
And decorate such views as mine.

To the fine steed you sportsmen bow,
But picturesque prefers a cow;
On her high hips and horned head
How true the light and shade are shed:
Indeed, I should prefer by half,
To a fine colt, a common calf;
The un-shorn sheep, the shaggy goat,
The ass with rugged, ragged coat,
Would to a taste-inspired mind,
Leave the far-famed Eclipse behind:
In a grand stable he might please,
But ne'er should graze beneath my trees."

Caught by his words, the northern 'Squire
Failed not his learning to admire:
But yet he had a wish to quiz
The Doctor's humour, and his phiz.
"I have a house," he said, "at hand,
Where you my service may command;
There I have cows, and asses too,
And pigs, and sheep, Sir, not a few;
Where you, at your untroubled leisure,
May draw them as it suits your pleasure.
You shall be welcome with your mare,
And find a country 'Squire's fare:
If a few days with us you pass,—
We'll give you meat—and give her grass."
Thus 'twas agreed; they came on shore,
The party sauntered on before;
But, ere they reached the mansion fair,
Grizzle had borne her master there.

It was indeed a pleasant spot
That this same country 'Squire had got;
And Syntax now the party joined
With salutation free and kind.

'SQUIRE.

"This, Doctor Syntax, is my sister:
Why, my good Sir, you have not kissed her."

SYNTAX.

"Do not suppose I'm such a brute
As to disdain the sweet salute."

'SQUIRE.

"And this, Sir, is my loving wife,
The joy and honour of my life."

SYNTAX.

"A lovely Lady to the view!
And with your leave, I'll kiss her too."

Thus pleasant words the converse cheered,
Till dinner on the board appeared;
Where the warm welcome gave a zest
To all the plenty of the feast.
The Doctor eat, and talked and quaffed;
The good Host smiled, the Ladies laughed.

'SQUIRE.

"As you disdain both fowl and fish,
Think you your art could paint that dish?"

SYNTAX.

"Though 'twill to hunger give relief,—
There's nothing picturesque in beef:

But there are artists—if you'll treat 'em;
Will paint your dinners; that is—eat 'em."

'SQUIRE.

"But sure your pencil might command
Whate'er is noble, vast and grand,—
The beasts, forsooth, of Indian land;
Where the fierce, savage tiger scowls,
And the fell, hungry lion growls."

SYNTAX.

"These beasts may all be subjects fit;
But, for their likeness, will they sit?
I'd only take a view askaunt,
From the tall back of elephant;
With half an hundred Indians round me,
That such sharp claws might not confound me.
But now, as we have ceased to dine,
And I have had my share of wine,
I should be glad to close the feast
By drawing some more harmless beast."

The Doctor found a quick consent,
And to the farm their way they bent.
A tub inverted, formed his seat;
The animals their painter meet:
Cows, asses, sheep, and ducks and geese,
Present themselves to grace the piece:
Poor Grizzle, too, among the rest,
Of the true picturesque possessed,
Quitted the meadow to appear,
And took her station in the rear:

The sheep all baaed, the asses brayed,
The moo-cows lowed, and Grizzle neighed!
"Stop, brutes," he cried, "your noisy glee;
I do not want to hear—but see;
Though by the picturesquish laws,
You're better too with open jaws."

The Doctor now, with genius big,
First drew a cow, and next a pig:
A sheep now on the paper passes,
And then he sketched a group of asses:
Nor did he fail to do his duty
In giving Grizzle all her beauty.
"And now," says Miss (a laughing elf),
"I wish, Sir, you would draw yourself."
"With all my heart," the Doctor said,
"But not with horns upon my head."
"And then I hope you'll draw my face."
"In vain, fair maid, my art would trace
Those winning smiles, that native grace.
The beams of beauty I disclaim;
The picturesque's my only aim:
My pencil's skill is mostly shown
In drawing faces like my own,
Where Time, alas! and anxious Care
Have placed so many wrinkles there."

Now all beneath a spreading tree
They chat, and sip their evening tea,
Where Syntax told his various fate;
His studious life and married state;

And that he hoped his Tour would tend
His comforts and his purse to mend.

At length they to the house retreated,
And round the supper soon were seated;
When the time quickly passed away,
And gay good humour closed the day.

CANTO XV.

"VIRTUE embraces every state;
And, while it gilds the rich and great,
It cheers their heart who humbly stray
Along Life's more sequestered way:
While, from beneath the portals proud,
Wealth oft relieves the suppliant crowd,
The wayworn pilgrim smiles to share,
In lowly homes, the welcome fare.
In splendid halls and painted bowers
Plenty may crown the festive hours;
Yet still within the secret dell
The hospitable Virtues dwell;
And in this Isle, so brave and fair,
Kind Charity is everywhere.
Within the city's ample bound
Her stately piles are seen around;
Where every want, and every pain
That in man's feeble nature reign,
Where the sad heir of pining grief
May, bless'd be Heaven! obtain relief:
While, on the humble village-green,
How oft the low-roofed pile is seen,
Where poverty forgets its woes,
And wearied age may find repose.

"Thrice happy Britons! while the car
Of furious, unrelenting War
Leaves the dire track of streaming gore
On many a hapless, distant shore,—
While a remorseless tyrant's hand
Deals misery through each foreign land,
And fell destruction, from the throne
To him who doth the cottage own,—
Peace beams upon your sea-girt Isle,
Where the bright virtues ever smile;
Where hostile shoutings ne'er molest
The happy inmate's genial rest.
Where'er it is his lot to go,
He will not meet an armed foe;
Nay, wheresoe'er his way doth tend,
He sure may chance to find a friend."

Thus, having rose at early day,
As through the fields he took his way,
The Doctor did his thoughts rehearse,
And, as the Muse inspired, in verse:
For, while with skill each form he drew,
His Reverence was a poet too.

But soon a bell's shrill, tinkling sound,
Re-echoed all the meads around,
And said as plain as bell could say—
"Breakfast is ready—come away."
The welcome summons he obeyed,
And found an arbour's pleasing shade,
Where, while the plenteous meal was
spread,
The woodbine flaunted o'er his head.

"Ah! little do the proud and great,
Amid the pomp and toil of state,
Know of those simple, real joys,
With which the bosom never cloys!
O! what a heart-reviving treat
I find within this rural seat!
All that can please the quickened taste,
Is offered in this fair repast.
The flowers, on their native bed,
Around delicious odours shed:
A bloom that with the floweret vies
On those fair cheeks, attracts my eyes;
And what sweet music greets my ear,
When that voice bids me welcome here!
Indeed, each sense combines to bless
The present hour of happiness."

Thus Syntax spoke, nor spoke in vain;
The Ladies felt the flattering strain;
Nor could they do enough to please
The Doctor for his courtesies.
"All that you see, if that's a charm,
Is, Sir, the produce of our farm:
The rolls are nice, our oven bakes 'em;
Those oat cakes too, my sister makes 'em.
The cream is rich, pray do not save it;
The brindled cow you drew, Sir, gave it:
And here is some fresh-gathered fruit—
I hope it will your palate suit:
'Tis country fare which you receive,
But 'tis the best we have to give.

"O!" said the 'Squire, "the Doctor jokes
With us poor harmless country folks:
I wonder that with all his sense,
And such a tickling eloquence,
He has not turned an humble priest
Into a good fat dean, at least.
We know how soon a Lady's ear
Will list the honeyed sound to hear:
At the same time, I'm free to say,
I think the men as vain as they.
How happens it, my learned friend,
That you have not attained your end?
That all your figures and your tropes
Have not fulfilled your rightful hopes?
I should suppose your shining parts,
And above all your flattering arts,
Would soon have turned your grizzly mare
Into a handsome chaise and pair.
I live amidst my native groves,
And the calm scene my nature loves;
But still I know, and often see,
What gains are made by flattery."

"That may be true," the Doctor said:
"But flattery is not my trade.
Indeed, dear Sir, you do me wrong—
No sordid interest guides my tongue;
Honour and Virtue I admire,
Or in a Bishop or a 'Squire;

But falsehood I most keenly hate,
Though gilt with wealth, or crowned with
state.
For *TRUTH* I'm like a lion bold;
And a base lie I never told:
Indeed, I know too many a sinner
Will lie by dozens for a dinner;
But, from the days of earliest youth,
I've worshipped, as I've practised Truth:
Nay, many a stormy, bitter strife
I've had with my dear, loving wife,
Who often says she might have seen
Her husband a fine, pompous Dean;
Indeed, she sometimes thinks her spouse
Might have a mitre on his brows,
If, putting scruples out of view,
He'd do as other people do.
No—I will never lie nor fawn,
Nor flatter to be robbed in lawn.
I too, can boast a certain rule
Within the precincts of my school:
Whatever faults I may pass by,
I never can forgive a lie.
I hate to use the birchen rod;
But, when a boy forswears his God;
When he in purposed falsehood deals,
My heavy strokes the culprit feels.
Vice I detest, whoever shows it,
And, when I see it, I'll expose it:
But, to kind hearts my homage due
I willing pay, and pay to you;

Nor will you, Sir, deny the share
That's due to these two Ladies fair."

The 'Squire replied, "I e'en must yield,
And leave you master of the field:
These Ladies will, I'm sure, agree
That you have fairly conquered me:
But, be assured, all joke apart,
I feel your doctrine from my heart.
Your free-born conduct I commend,
And shall rejoice to call you friend;
O! how it would my spirits cheer
If you were but the rector here.
Our Parson, I'm concerned to say,
Had rather drink and game—than pray:
He makes no bones to curse and swear,
In any rout to take a share,
And what's still worse, he'll springe a
hare.
I wish his neck he would but break,
Or tumble drunk into the Lake!
For, know the Living's mine to give,
And you should soon the cure receive:
The Benefice, I'm sure is clear,
At least three hundred pounds a year."

"I thank you, Sir, with all my heart,"
Said Syntax, "but we now must part."
The fair ones cried—"We beg you'll stay,
And pass with us another day."
"—Ladies, I would 'twere in my power,
But I can't stay another hour:

I feel your kindness to my soul,
And wish I could my fate control:
Within ten days the time will come
When I shall be expected home;
Nor is this all—for, strange to say,
I must take London in my way."
Thus converse kind the moments cheered,
Till Grizzle at the gate appeared.
"Well," said the 'Squire, "since you must go,
Our hearty wishes we bestow:
And if your genius bids you take
Another journey to the Lake,
Remember *Worthy-Hall*, we pray,
And come and make a longer stay:
Write too, and tell your distant friends
With what success your journey ends.
We do not mean it as a bribe,
But to your work we must subscribe."
The Ladies, too, exclaimed—"Repeat
Your visit to our northern seat."

Poor Syntax knew not how to tell
The gratitude he felt so well:
And, when at length he said—"Good bye,"
A tear was bright in either eye.

The Doctor paced along the way
Till it drew nigh the close of day,
When the fair town appeared in sight,
Where he proposed to pass the night:

But as he reached the destined Inn,
The landlord, with officious grin,
At once declared he had no bed
Where Syntax could repose his head:
At least, where such a reverend guest
Would think it fit to take his rest:
A main of cocks had fought that day,
And all the gentry chose to stay.
"Observe, my friend, I mind not cost,"
Says Syntax to his cringing host;
"But still, at least, I may be able
To sleep with Grizzle in a stable;
And many a Doctor after all,
Is proud to *slumber in a stall:*
In short, I only want to sleep
Where neither rogue nor knave can creep:
I travel not with change of coats,
But in these bags are all my notes:
Which, should I lose, would prove my ruin,
And be for ever, my undoing."

Thus as he spoke, a lively blade,
With dangling queue and smart cockade,
Replied at once, "I have a room;
The friend I looked for is not come;
And of two beds where we may rest,
You, my good Sir, shall have the best:
So you may sleep without alarm:
No living wight shall do you harm:
You may depend upon my word;
I serve the King, and wear a sword."

"Your offer, Sir, I kindly greet,"
Says Syntax, "but you'll let me treat
With what is best to drink and eat;
And I request you will prepare,
To your own taste, the bill of fare."

The Doctor and the Captain sat,
Till tired of each other's chat,
They both agreed it would be best
To seek the balmy sweets of rest.
Syntax soon closed his weary eye,
Nor thought of any danger nigh:
While, like the ever-watchful snake,
His sharp companion lay awake,
Impatient to assail his prey;
When, soon as it was dawn of day,
He gently seized the fancied store;
But, as he passed the creaking door,
Syntax awoke, and saw the thief;
When, loudly bawling for relief,
He forward rushed in naked state,
And caught the culprit at the gate:
Against that gate his head he beat,
Then kicked him headlong to the street.

The ostler from his bed arose,
In time to hear and see the blows.
Says Syntax, "I'll not make a riot;
I've saved my notes, and I'll be quiet.
The rascal, if I'm not mistaken,
Will ask his legs to save his bacon:

But what a figure I appear!
I must not stand and shiver here:
So take me back into the room,
From whence in this strange way I've
 come."
The ostler then the Doctor led
To the warm comforts of his bed:
Into that bed he quickly crept,
Beneath his head his bags he kept,
And on that pillow safely slept.

CANTO XVI.

Fair Virtue is its own reward,
For Heaven remains its constant guard;
And it becomes us all to trust
In this grand truth—that Heaven is just.
Whatever forms the human lot,
Whether in palace or in cot,
In the calm track or frequent strife,
Man leads his variegated life;
Whether he feasts his smiling hours
In stately halls or painted bowers;
Whether he labours through the day
In Winter cold, or Summer's ray;
Or, in long nights of torturing pain,
He strives to close his eyes in vain;
Comfort will on his lot attend
If Virtue be his bosom friend.
In youth, when Love's creative power
Forms the young Passion's roseate bower;
When, life matured, the eager game
That hunts for wealth or seeks for fame,
Is subtly played, with various art,
To seize the mind and fill the heart:
When Pleasure doth its charms display,
And Syrens sing but to betray;
If Virtue's called, it will defy
The attack of every enemy.

When age comes on with stealing pace,
And the crutch marks the closing race,
Virtue supports her champion's cause,
And cheers him with her fond applause;
Nay, e'en at Death's resistless hour,
She still displays a conscious power;
Nor fails to make the flowerets bloom
Round the dark confines of the tomb.

Thus Syntax pondered—when around
His head he turned, and grateful found
His bags and notes all safe and sound:
Pleased with the prospect, he was fain
To yawn, and go to sleep again.

But, while he still enjoyed his dream,
His story was the general theme
Of every tongue, and made a din
Through all the purlieus of the Inn.
The ostler told it to the maid,
And she the whole, and more betrayed;
Nay, in her idle, eager prate,
Mistook the window for the gate:
For, though she lay all snug and quiet,
And slept unconscious of the riot,
She swore that, all within her view,
The Parson from the window threw
A full-grown man into the street,
Who haply lighted on his feet,
And then ran off through all the dirt,
With night-cap on and half a shirt.

The Barber caught the story next,
Who stuck no closer to the text:
But left a face half-shaved, and ran
To tell it to the Clergyman.
"O! bless me, Sir," he cried, "I fear
To utter, what you now must hear:
At the *Blue Bell* there's been such doing—
The house, I'm certain, it must ruin;
Nay, as I live, I'll tell no further,—
A Bishop has committed murther!
He seized a Captain by the pate,
And dashed it so against the gate,
That all the planks are covered o'er
With scattered brains and human gore!
His Lordship gave him such a banging,
That he will scarce escape with hanging.
They quarrelled, Sir, as it was said,
About the colours black and red;
The Captain manfully professed
That the bright scarlet was the best;
And they, who that fine colour wore,
The first of all professions bore;
While black (it was not very civil)
Was the known livery of the devil.
Thus soon a loud dispute arose,
Which from hard words went on to blows;
And ended in this bloody strife,
Which robbed the Captain of his life:
And, if fair justice does not falter,
She'll deck the Bishop with a halter."
The Parson smiled, and bid the calf
Go home and shave the other half:

But when he came, the lathered elf
Had shaved the other half himself.

The Taylor laid aside his needle
To hear the story from the Beadle,
Who swore he had strange news to tell
Of what had happened at the *Bell:*
"Would you believe it, that, last night,
A highwayman, a man of might,
Down in his bed a Lawyer bound,
And robbed him of a thousand pound;
Then gagged him that he might not rouse
The people sleeping in the house."
"No, no," says Snip, "however strong,
No gag will stop a Lawyer's tongue;
And, after all, the stolen pelf
Is what, I'm sure, he stole himself;
For, if the real truth we knew,
He's the worst villain of the two!
They're thieves in grain—they never alter—
Attorneys all deserve a halter.
If that is all, I'll mind my stitches,
Nor lay aside John Bumkin's breeches."

The Blacksmith, while a traveller stayed
That a new horse-shoe might be made,
Informed him that a reverend Clerk
Last night was strangled in the dark,
No one knew how—'twas at the *Bell,*
The murderer not a soul could tell.
The Justice though would make a rout,
And try to find the fellow out.—

Thus Rumour spread the simple case,
In every form throughout the place.

The Doctor now unclosed his eyes,
And thought that it was time to rise:
So up he got, and down he went,
To scold the Landlord fully bent;
Who, pale, and trembling with affright
At what had happened in the night,
Approached with such an humble look,
The Doctor's rage at once forsook
His Christian breast; and, with a voice
That did the poor man's heart rejoice,
He bid him soon as he was able,
To let the coffee grace the table.
"I do aver," the Landlord said,
"That since I've carried on my trade,
Since I've been master of the *Bell*,
As all throughout the town can tell,
(And that is now ten years or more)
I ne'er knew such mishap before.
The fellow, Sir, upon my word,
Let loose his money like a Lord.
I receive all who come this way,
And care not, Sir, how long they stay,
So they but eat and drink—and pay.
I ask not from whence people come,
What is their name, or where their home.
That he's a rogue I think is clear,
Nor e'er again shall enter here.
He is some sharper, I suppose,
Who round about the country goes:

While to assist his lawless game,
He takes the soldier's noble name.
I understand the rogue you banged,
And in good time, Sir, he'll be hanged:
I hope that all your notes you've found,—
I'm told they're worth a thousand pound."
"Prove that," says Syntax, "my dear honey,
And I will give you half the money.
Think not, my friend, I'm such a fool,
That I have been so late at school,
To put my bank-notes in a bag
That hangs across my Grizzle nag;
No, they were notes to make a book;
The thief my meaning, friend, mistook;
For know the man would not have found
Them worth—to him—a single pound:
Though much I hope that they will be
The source of many a pound to me."
Thus Syntax cheered the Landlord's heart
Till the time warned him to depart;
When soon along the beaten road,
Poor Grizzle bore her reverend load.

The Doctor's pleasant thoughts beguile
The journey onward many a mile;
For many a mile he had not seen
But one unvarying, level green;
Nor had the way one object brought
That waked a *picturesquish* thought.
A spire, indeed, across the down,
Seemed to denote a neighbouring town;

And that he viewed with some delight—
For there he hoped to pass the night.

A farmer now, so blithe and gay,
Came trotting briskly on his way.
"Will you," says Syntax, "tell me, friend,
If to yon town this way doth tend?"
"This road, good Sir, will take you there;
You're surely going to the fair;
'Tis the first mart both far and near,
For horses, cows, and such like gear;
And, from the beast I've in my eye,
You're going, Sir, a nag to buy:
I think, if I the truth may tell,
You have not got a nag to sell;
For not a person in the fair
Will give ten shillings for your mare."
Syntax, who dearly loved a joke,
And long had lived 'mong country folk,
Thought he could work a little mirth
Out of this rustic son of earth;
So thus the conversation flowed,
As they jogged on the beaten road.

SYNTAX.

"Believe me, Farmer, long together,
In sunshine, and in stormy weather,
My mare and I have trotted on,
Nor is as yet our labour done:
And, though her figure you despise,
Did you but know her qualities,

You would not rate her quite so low
As now you seem disposed to do."

FARMER.

"I'll lay a pound, if you are willing,
She does not fetch you twenty shilling."

SYNTAX.

"First, my good friend, one truth I'll tell;—
I do not want my mare to sell:
While to lay wagers I am loth:
The practice would disgrace my cloth:
Nor ever, while Life's path I trace,
Will I my sacred rank disgrace:
But yet I think you under-rate
Poor Grizzle's qualities and state.
'Tis true, she's past the age of beauty;
Yet still the old girl does her duty;
And some one surely will be found
To think, at least she's worth a pound:
Nay, to amuse the country folk,
We'll put her up, by way of joke,
But no one must the wager smoke:
And I propose, that if you lose,
(No Christian will the bet refuse)
The money to the poor you'll give,
'Twill be a Christian donative:
And if my old and faithful mare
Should be so treated in the fair,
That not a person would be willing
To offer for her twenty shilling,

On honour I will do the same,
As sure as Syntax is my name.
Such are the terms that I propose,
So let us now the bargain close."
"Give me your hand," the farmer said,
"The terms I'll keep, the bargain's made."
Thus they rode on and reached the town:—
The pipe and bowl the evening crown.

The morrow came, and through the fair
The Farmer led the grizzle mare.
Says one, "I would not bid a pound;
She's only fit to feed a hound;
But would a hound the gift receive,
For she has nought but bones to give?
Where must we look her ears to find?
And faith! she's left her tail behind!"
"Why," says another, "view her scars:
She must have left them in the wars."

As a warm Yeoman passed along,
He heard the jeerings of the throng,
And felt a strong desire to know
What pleased the laughing people so.
"A Parson, Sir," says one, "distressed,
Would sell that poor, that wretched beast;
And asks, I hear, a pound or two:
I think he'll ne'er get that from you."
"If that's the case," the Yeoman said,-
"I'll ease his heart, and buy the jade.
I'll bid two pounds, my friend, that's
plain,
And give him back his beast again."

The Farmer owned the wager lost,
And oped his bag to pay the cost:
"No, Sir," says Syntax, "'tis to you
To pay where'er you think it due:
But, as we passed the Common o'er,
I saw beside a cottage door,
A woman with a spinning-wheel,
Who turned her thread around the reel,
While joyful frolicked by her side
Three children, all in Nature's pride;
And I resign it to your care
To leave the welcome bounty there."

The Yeoman, when he heard the joke,
In friendly words to Syntax spoke.
"I, Sir, an humble mansion own,
About five furlongs from the town;
And there your Reverence I invite
To go and dine and pass the night.
To-day I give an annual feast,
Where you will be a welcome guest.
I love the cloth,—and humbly crave
That we may there your blessing have.
Come then, and bring your mare along;
Come, share the feast, and hear the song;
And in the evening will be seen
The merry dancers on the green."
"With joy," said Syntax, "I receive
The invitation which you give;
In your kind feast I'll bear a part,
And bring with me a grateful heart."

"I," said the Yeoman, "must be gone:
But shall expect you, Sir, at one."
Nor did the Doctor long delay:
To the farm-house he took his way;
And changed the bustle of the fair,
For a kind, noiseless welcome there.

CANTO XVII.

Ye Courtesies of life, all hail!
Whether along the peaceful vale,
Where the thatched cot alone is seen,
The humble mansion of the green,
Or in the city's crowded way,
Man—mortal man, is doomed to stray;
You give to joy an added charm,
And woe of half its pangs disarm.
How much in every state he owes
To what kind Courtesy bestows;
To that benign engaging art
Which decorates the human heart,
And, free from jealousy and strife,
Gilds all the charities of life.
To every act it gives a grace;
It adds a smile to every face;
And Goodness' self we better see
When dressed by gentle Courtesy.

Thus Syntax, as the house he sought,
Indulged the grateful, pleasing thought
And soon he stepped the threshold o'er,
Where the good Farmer went before:
Plenty appeared, and many a guest
Attended on the welcome feast.

The Doctor then, with solemn face,
Proceeded to the appointed place,
And, in due form, pronounced the grace.
That thankful ceremony done,
The fierce attack was soon begun;
While meat and pudding, fowl and fish,
All vanished from each ample dish.
The dinner o'er, the bowl appeared:
The enlivening draughts the spirits cheered;
Nor did the pleasant Doctor fail,
Between the cups of foaming ale,
To gain the laugh by many a tale.
But it so happed—among the rest—
The Farmer's Landlord was a guest;
A buckish blade, who kept a horse,
To try his fortune on the course;
Was famous for his fighting cocks,
And his staunch pack to chase the fox:
Indeed, could he a booby bite,
He'd play at cards throughout the night;
Nor was he without hopes to get
Syntax to make some silly bet.
"I never bet," the Doctor said,
While a deep frown his thoughts betrayed:
"Your gold I do not wish to gain,
And mine shall in my purse remain:
No tempting card, no gambling art,
Shall make it from my pocket start.
Gaming, my worthy Sir, I hate;
It neither suits my means nor state:

'Tis the worst passion, I protest,
That's known to haunt the human breast!
Of all vile habitudes the worst;
The most delusive and accurst;
And, if you please, I'll lay before you
A very melancholy story;
Such as, I think, will ring your heart,
And wound you in the tenderest part;
That will in striking colours show
The bitter pangs—the bitter woe,
That do, too oft, from gaming flow."
"Nay," said the 'Squire, "I don't deny
I often like my luck to try;
And no one here, I'm sure, will say
That when I lose I do not pay:
But as you think it such a sin,
Pray try to cure me—and begin."

SYNTAX.

"How many of the human kind,
Who, to their common honour blind,
Look not in any path to stray
But where fell Passion leads the way;
Who, born to every real claim
To wear the fairest wreath of Fame,
Reject the good by Nature given,
And scoff at every boon of Heaven!
Yes; such there are, and such we find
At every point that gives the wind:
But, when among the crowd we see
One whom, in prodigality,

Fortune and Nature had combined
To fill his purse and form his mind;
Whose manly strength is graced with ease,
And has the happy power to please;
Whose cooler moments never heard
The frantic vow to Heaven preferred;
And near whose steps Repentance bears
The vase of purifying tears;
When such a victim we behold,
Urged by the rampant lust of gold,
Yielding his health, his life, his fame,
As offerings to the god of game;
The tear grows big in Virtue's eye,
Pale Reason heaves the poignant sigh;
The guardian spirit turns away,
And hell enjoys a holiday.

"Is there on earth a hellish vice?
There is, my friend, 'tis avarice:
Has avarice a more hellish name?
It has, my friend—the lust of game.
All this, perhaps, you'll thus deny:—
'There's no one, with more grace than I,
Lets shillings drop and guineas fly!
To the dejected hapless friend
My door I ope, my purse I lend;
To purchase joy my wealth I give,
And like a man of fashion live.'
—This may be true—but still your breast
Is with the love of gold possessed.
Why watch whole nights the fatal card,
Or look to dice for your reward?

Why risk your real wealth with those
Whom you know not, and no one knows;
With maggots whom foul Fortune's ray
Has raised from dunghills into day;
Who would in your misfortune riot,
And seek your ruin for their diet?
Pleasure it cannot be, for pains
Will mingle with your very gains—
Will hover round the golden store,
Which, ere the passing moment's o'er,
May, horrid chance! be yours no more.

"As yet, you cannot use the plea
Of beggared men—necessity;
Plenty as yet adorns your board,
And numerous vassals own you Lord:
Your woods look fair—their trunks in-
crease,
The Hamadryades live in peace;
But cards and dice, more powerful far
That e'en the sharpest axes are;
At one dire stroke have oft been found
To level forests with the ground:
Have seized the mansion's lofty state,
And turned its master from the gate.

"A youth, in wealth and fashion bred,
But by the love of gaming led,
Soon found that ample wealth decay;
Farm after farm was played away,
Till, the sad history to complete,
His park, his lawns, his ancient seat.

Were all in haste and hurry sold,
To raise the heaps of ready gold.
They, like the rest, soon passed away,
The villain's gain, the sharper's prey;
While he, alas! resolved to shun
The arts by which he was undone,
Sought, by hard labour, to sustain
His weary life of woe and pain;
But Nature soon refused to give
The strength by which he strove to live;
And nought was left him but to try
What casual pity would supply;
To stray where chance or hunger led,
And humbly ask for scanty bread.
One day, to his despairing eyes,
He saw a stately mansion rise:
Nor looked he long before he knew
Each wood and copse that round it grew;
For all the scene that seemed so fair,
Once knew in his a master's care.
Struck with the sight, and sore oppressed,
He sought a bank whereon to rest;
There long he lay, and sighed his grief;
Tears came—but did not bring relief.
At last he took his tottering way
Where once he loved so well to stray,
And, pressed by hunger, sought the gate
Where suppliant Want was used to wait—
Where suppliant Want was ne'er denied
The morsel left by glutted Pride.
But, ah! those generous times were o'er,
And suppliant Want relieved no more.

The mastiff growled—the liveried thief
With insolence denied relief:—
The wretch, dissolving in a groan,
Turned from the portal, once his own:
But ere he turned, he told his name,
And cursed once more the love of game;
Then sought the lawn, for Nature failed,
And sorrow o'er his strength prevailed.
Beneath an oak's wide-spreading shade
His weary limbs he careless laid;
Then called on Heaven;—(the bitter prayer
Of Misery finds admittance there!)
And ere the sun with parting ray,
Had heightened the last blush of day,
Sunk and worn out with want and grief,
He found in death a kind relief.

"The oak records the doleful tale,
Which makes the conscious reader pale;
And tells—'In this man's fate behold
The love of play—the lust of gold.'
No moral, Sir, I shall impart;
I trust you feel it in your heart.

"'You're young,' you'll say, 'and must engage
In the amusements of the age.'
Go then, and let your mountain bare
The forest's verdant livery wear;
Let Parian marble grace your hall,
And Titian glow upon your wall;

Its narrow channels boldly break,
And swell your rivulet to a lake:
To richer harvests bend your soil,
While labour fattens in the toil:
Encourage Nature, and impart
The half-transparent veil of Art.
Let Music charm your melting breast,
And soothe each passion into rest:
Let Genius from your hand receive
The bounty that can make it live;
And call the Muses from on high,
To give you immortality.
To these the hardy pleasures join,
Where Exercise and Health combine:
At the first opening of the morn,
O'er hill and dale, with hound and horn,
Boldly pursue the subtle prey,
And share the triumphs of the day:
Nor let the evening hours roll
Unaided by the social bowl:
Nor should fair Friendship be away,
But crown with smiles the festive day.
Say, need I add the joys they prove
Who live in bonds of virtuous love?
Where fond affection fills the heart,
The baser passions shall depart.
While the babe hangs on Beauty's breast,
While in a parent's arms caressed,
Each low-bred thought, all vicious aims,
The pure domestic mind disclaims.
Virtue inspires his every sense,
Who looks on cherub innocence:—

Then seek a shield 'gainst passion's strife
In the calm joys of wedded life.

"This is to live, and to enjoy
Those pleasures which our pains destroy:
This is to live, and to receive
The praises which the good will give:
This is to make that use of wealth
Which heightens e'en the flush of health;
Improves the heart, and gives a claim
To a fair, fragrant wreath of Fame."

"I thank you, Sir," the Farmer said;—
"'Tis a sad tale you have displayed.
How I the poor man's lot deplore!
The more I think, I feel the more:
And much I wish my Landlord too
Would keep his wretched fate in view;
But while my poor good woman weeps,
Behold how very sound he sleeps.
I beg that we may change the scene,
And join the dancers on the green."
Sal now exclaimed, "The people say
Ralph is so drunk he cannot play."
"Then I'll be Fiddler," Syntax cried;
"By me his place shall be supplied!
Ne'er fear, my lasses, you shall soon
Be ambling to some pretty tune,
And in a measured time shall beat
The green sod with your nimble feet.
While Virtue o'er your pleasure reigns,
You're welcome to my merry strains;

While Virtue smiles upon your joy,
I'll gladly my best skill employ;
For, sure, 'twill give me great delight
To be your Fiddler through the night.
I know full well I do not err
From any point of character:
To Heaven I cannot give offence
While I enliven innocence:
For thus to Virtuous man 'tis given
To dance, and sing, and go to Heaven.
Your merry minstrelsy prolong,
And to your dances add the song:
E'en while you caper, loudly sing
In honour of your noble King."

CHORUS OF PEASANTS.

"Strike, strike the lyre! awake the sounding shell!
How happy we who in these valleys dwell!
How blest we live beneath his gentle sway,
Whom mighty realms and distant seas obey!
Make him, propitious Heaven! your choicest care!
O make him happy as his people are!"

'Twas thus they fiddled, danced, and sung;
With harmless glee the village rung:
At length dull midnight bid them close
A day of joy, with calm repose.

CANTO XVIII.

Let Grandeur blush, and think how few
Of all the many-coloured crew,
The motley group of fools and knaves,
Who hourly prove themselves its slaves,
However Fashion gilds the dress,
Attain the expected happiness!
Let Grandeur blush, and blushing own
How seldom is to greatness known,
That pure and unimbittered lot
Which often cheers the peasant's cot;
The hallowed bliss, the nameless charm
That decorates the fertile farm.

Thus Syntax pondered as his eye
Surveyed the cheerful family:
Who round the breakfast-table seated,
With one accord his entrance greeted:
At the same time, they all expressed
Much sorrow that their reverend guest
Had ordered Grizzle to the door
In order to pursue his Tour.
"Doctor, I'm grieved so soon to part,"
Burst from the Yeoman's friendly heart;
"Yet hope, whene'er you this way come,
You'll not forget this is your home:—

You see how we poor farmers live,—
A welcome's all we have to give;
But that's sincere—so come and try."
A few kind words were the reply.

Syntax once more his beast bestrode:
He bade farewell, and off he rode.

Now Nature's beauties caught his eye,
Arrayed in gay simplicity;
And as he passed the road along,
The blackbird's note, the thrush's song,
With musical and native mirth,
Seemed to do homage to his worth:
The varied landscape here combined
To fascinate the eye and mind,
To charm the gazer's every sense
From the commanding eminence.
The expanding plain, with plenty crowned,
Diffuses health and fragrance round;
While, on a lofty, craggy height,
A castle rises to the sight,
Which in its day of strength and pride,
The arms of threatening foes defied.
Beneath the mouldering abode
In mazy course a rivulet flowed;
And, free from the tempestuous gale,
Its silent stream refreshed the vale:
The vale the scattered hamlet cheered,
And many a straw-roof'd cot appeared;
While smiling groups at every door
Spoke grief a stranger to the poor.

With pious thought and eye serene,
Syntax surveyed the enchanting scene,
And thus in grateful mood began:
"So deals the Omnipotent with man.
Such are thy gifts, all-gracious Power,
To us, the creatures of an hour!
And yet how oft we barter these,
How oft we risk our health and ease,
Thy best bequest, thy choicest treasure,
For follies which we misname pleasure:
And slaves to vanity and art,
Check the best feelings of the heart.—
How the scene charms the ravished eye:
I cannot, will not, pass it by!"
He said,—and from his pocket took
His pencil, and his sketching book;
While Grizzle, in contented mood,
Close by her busy master stood:
When, clouds of dust proclaimed the
approach
Of something Syntax deemed a coach.
Four wheels in truth it had to boast,
Although what it resembled most
Were hard to say:—suffice, this *tub*
Was built in London, where a club,
Yclept *Four-horse*, is now the rage,
And famed for whims in equipage.
Dashers! who once a month assemble;
Make creditors and coachmen tremble:
And, dressed in colours vastly fine,
Drive to some public-house to dine:

There game, and drink, and swear, and
then—
Drive in disorder back again.

Now Syntax, with some kind of fear,
Beheld the vehicle draw near;
And, like her master, Grizzle too
Was far from happy at the view;
For a long whip had caught her eye,
Moving about most rapidly;
Though little thought the hapless nag,
The joke which the exalted wag,
Who held the reins with skilful hand,
Against both mare and master planned.
But now the curious Doctor spied
The emblem of Patrician pride,
Which on the pannels of the coach,
Proclaimed a noble Lord's approach:
Nay, (for the facts will plainly prove it)
It was a noble Lord who drove it:
For 'tis well known to men of rank,
That Lords will sometimes play a prank,
And thus indulge themselves in jokes
As low as those of vulgar folks.
But 'tis not easy to express
The wild surprise, the deep distress,
Which Syntax felt, when this same Lord
Aimed at his back the flaunting cord;
And when the whip, with skilful turn
Was well applied to Grizzle's stern;
That stern, enough to make one shudder,
Which we all know had lost its rudder;

Her rage appeared in either eye,
And then she neighed indignantly.
Such seemed she as when erst she bore
A trumpeter to fields of gore;
When, in the battle's heat, at large,
She led whole squadrons to the charge;
While Syntax, as she scoured the plain,
Indulged the moralizing strain.
"Can I in this foul conduct scan
The Peer, or well-bred Gentleman?
Or rather must not Virtue frown
On such a high-born, titled clown?
Thus, then, do Nobles play the fool?
A conduct which in my poor school,
If 'mong my boys it dare appear;
If they should ape that monkey there;
They for their fun should pay full dearly;
I'd whip the blackguards most severely.
But I'll not waste another word
Upon this vulgar, booby Lord;
For I have something else to do,
And Grizzle, what's become of you?"
A farmer's well-stored barn, hard by,
Attracted her observing eye,
Where many a truss of fragrant hay
Induced the prudent beast to stay.
Meanwhile, her discontented master,
Reflecting on the late disaster,
Paced slowly on, brimful of care,
And wondered who had got his mare.
Indeed he feared she might be found
Within the precincts of a pound;

But soon his quadruped he saw,
Up to her girths in hay and straw;
While he, who owned the neighbouring
farm,
Prepared to raise his weighty arm;
And, having just observed the theft,
Brandished a horsewhip right and left,
(Alas! it cannot be denied,)
To lay about on Grizzle's hide.
Syntax beheld the harsh intent:
"Forbear," he cried, "the punishment!
Why make her feel the chastening thong?
She knows not she is doing wrong.
Forgive my warmth, but truly, Sir,
This suits not with the character
Of one who treads on British ground,
A land for justice so renowned:
I'll pay for all the straw that's wasted,
And all the hay that she has tasted:
Your courtesy I now invoke,
So name the cost, and spare the stroke."

The Farmer paused—as by a charm—
And dropped at once the uplifted arm:
"Forgive me, Sir, for what," he cried,
"Cannot, indeed, be justified:
But for my haste, I'll make amends:
And let us now, good Sir, be friends;
That is my house:—you'll enter there,
And, Thomas, take the Doctor's mare.
Come, reverend Sir, I'll lead the way:"
The Doctor did not disobey,

And soon was met with welcome glee,
By all the Farmer's family.
At length some business of the day
Summoned the honest host away:
So Syntax thought he'd look about,
To find some curious object out:
When, lo! a dairy met his view,
Where, full of cream, in order due,
The pans, the bowls, the jugs were placed,
Which tempted the Divine to taste.
But he found something better there:
A village damsel young and fair
Attracted his admiring eye;
Who, as he entered, heaved a sigh.
Now Syntax, as we all must know,
Ne'er heard a sigh or tale of woe,
But instant wished to bring relief,
To dry the tear and soothe the grief.
"Come here, sweet girl," he softly said;
"Tell me your cares—nor be afraid:
Come here, and seat you by my side;
You'll find in me a friendly guide.
Relate your sorrows,—tell the truth;
What is it? does some perjured youth
Unfaithful to his promise prove,
Nor make the fond return of love?
'Tis so, I see; but raise your eye:
On me, my pretty girl, rely:
You have my tenderest sympathy.
Again, I say, your grief impart;
You've gained an interest in my heart:

For well I know the pangs they prove
Who grieve for unrequited love."

The listening mother, who had heard
Love talked of, kindled at the word;
And, rushing in, expressed her rage:—
"For shame! for shame! while hoary age
Whitens your head, I see your eye
Is beaming with iniquity.
Begone, you old, you wanton goat,
Your heart is black as is your coat!
A Parson too! may Heaven forgive
The wicked age in which we live!
I'll go and tell my honest spouse
The snake he harbours in his house:
He'll give such hypocrites their due,
I'll warrant it;" and off she flew.

The Host arrived, but by that time
The false alarm, the imputed crime,
Nancy had ventured to unfold,
And mother now had ceased to scold:
While, the rude anger turned to mirth,
They all confess the Doctor's worth.

Dinner was soon upon the table,
And Grizzle feeding in the stable;
While joyful Syntax, once again,
Forgot past accidents and pain;
And, when night came, reposed his head
In peace, upon the welcome bed:

But ne'er did he to sleep consign
His weary limbs, till to the shrine
Of Heaven, he had addressed the prayer
Which ever finds admittance there.

CANTO XIX.

THE Sun arose in all its pride!
"Hail the bright orb," the Doctor cried,
"That makes the distant mountains glow,
And clears the misty vales below!
O! let me bless the Power divine
That bade its splendid fires to shine,
Invigorating warmth to give
To all that grow, and all that live:
Which, in the bowels of the earth,
Brings the rich metal into birth;
Or, piercing through the secret mine,
Makes rubies blush, and diamonds shine:
While man, the first, the head of all
That breathes upon this earthly ball,
As freely feels its force as they
Of insect tribe, who, in its ray,
Pass their short hour, and pass away.
O, what a picture greets my sight!
How my heart revels in delight,
While I behold the advancing day
O'er the wide scene its power display!
While, as I gaze, the enchanted eye
Drinks in the rich variety!
How the gleam brightens yonder tower!
How deep the shade within the bower!

The spreading oak and elm between,
How fine those blushes intervene!
Those brilliant lights!—they would demand
Claude's pencil, or a Titian's hand!
E'en while the distant hills I view,
Their orient colours change to blue.
The stream, within whose silver wave,
Poets might see the Naiads lave,
Now, lost in shade, no more is seen
To flow among the alders green:
But, let the eye its course pursue,
Again it brightens in the view:
Reflecting as its current flows,
Each flower that on the margin blows.
"Hail, favoured casement! where the sight
Is courted to enjoy delight;
To ascend the hill, and trace the plain,
Where lavish Nature's proud to reign!
Unlike those pictures that impart
The windows of Palladian art,
From whence no other object's seen
But gravel-walk, or shaven green;
Planned by the artist on his desk;
Pictures that are not *picturesque*.
But I should not perform my duty
Did I relinquish all this beauty;
Nor snatch, from this expansive view,
Some pretty little scene or two.
"The cot that's all bewhitened o'er,
With children playing at the door:

A peasant hanging o'er the hatch,
And the vine mantling on the thatch;
While the thick coppice, down the hill
Throws its green umbrage o'er the rill,
Whose stream drives on the busy mill,
In pleasing group their forms combine,
And suit a pencil such as mine.
Nor shall I miss the branchy screen
Of those fine elms that hide the green,
O'er which the tapering spire is seen.
I'll add no more—for to my mind,
The scene's complete—and well designed.
There are, indeed, who would insert
Those pigs which wallow in the dirt;
And though I hold a pig is good
Upon a dish, prepared for food,
I do not fear to say the brute
Does not my taste in painting suit;
For I most solemnly aver,
That he from genuine taste must err,
Who flouts at grace or character;
And there's as much in my old wig
As can be found about a pig.
For, to say truth, I don't inherit
This self-same *picturesquish* spirit,
That looks to nought but what is rough,
And ne'er thinks Nature coarse enough.
Their system does my genius shock,
Who see such graces in a dock;
Whose eye the *picturesque* admires
In straggling brambles, and in briers;

Nay, can a real beauty see
In a decayed and rotten tree.
I hate with them the trim of Art;
But from this rule I'll ne'er depart;—
In grandame Nature's vast collection,
To make a fair and fit selection,
Which, when in happy contrast joined,
Delights the informed, well-judging mind."

But lo! the Farmer, at the gate,
Proclaimed aloud the hour of eight;
And Syntax now in haste descends
To join his kind, expecting friends.

"Well," said his host, "another day
I trust your Reverence will stay."
"I thank you for the offer made,
But it can't be," the Doctor said:
"I have a weary way to go,
And much to see, and more to know;
Indeed so far I've got to roam,
A fortnight scarce will take me home;
And thanking you for all your care,
I must beg leave to seek my mare."
Grizzle was quickly to be found;
And, as the good folks stood around,
Syntax thought proper to discourse
Upon the virtues of his horse;
Nor did he fail at large to tell
That she had served him passing well;
While he forgot not to bewail
Her loss of ears and loss of tail:

But though among the passing folk,
His beast created many a joke,
And though the foul and sad disaster
Oft forced a laugh against the master,
They should not part while he was able
To keep himself and keep a stable;
Nay, to the last he'd cut and carve,
That his poor Grizzle might not starve.
Thus, as his history he recounted,
Into the saddle up he mounted,
And there for sometime having sat,
He closed at length his farewell chat.
He thought it best to avoid caressing:
So gave no kiss, but gave his blessing.
—On home, on book, on fame, intent,
The Doctor pondered as he went:
At night he looked his papers o'er,
And added to the learned store:
But the next morn, another scene,
The vast expanse of liquid green,
The ocean's self—broke on his eye,
In inexpressive majesty.
There, as he looked, full many a sail
Gave its white canvas to the gale,
And many a freighted vessel bore
Its treasure to the British shore.
When, as he traced the winding coast,
In praise and admiration lost,
Uprising in the distant view,
Half-seen through the ethereal blue,
A city's stately form appeared;
Upon the shore the mass was reared,

With glistening spires, while below
Masts like a forest seemed to grow.
'Twas Liverpool, that splendid mart,
Imperial London's counterpart,
Where wandering Mersey's rapid streams
Rival the honours of the Thames,
And bear on each returning tide,
Whate'er by commerce is supplied;
Whate'er the winds can hurry o'er
From every clime and distant shore.
Thus Syntax paced along the strand,
Through this fine scene of sea and land.
But nearer now the town appears,
The hum of men salutes his ears:
And soon, amid the noisy din,
He found the comforts of an Inn.
He eat, he drank, his pipe he smoked,
And with the Landlord quaintly joked;
But ere he slept he passed an hour
In adding something to his Tour;
Then sought his couch, in hopes the morn
Would with new thoughts the page adorn.
The morning came—he sallied out
To breathe the air, and look about.
Where'er he turned, his every sense
Grasped one vast scene of opulence:
In all he saw there was displayed
The proud magnificence of trade.

Syntax, an humble scholar bred,
With nought but learning in his head;

Profound, indeed, in classic art,
And goodness reigning in his heart,
Yet forty pounds a year was all
He could his fixed revenue call:
For which, on every Sabbath-day,
He went eight miles to preach and pray.
His school too, brought but little gains,
And scarce repaid him for his pains;
It gave, 'tis true, to drink and eat,
It furnished him with bread and meat,
And kept the wolf without the door,
But Syntax still was very poor.
His wife, indeed, had got the art,
To keep herself a little smart,
Yet he, good man, was always seen
With scanty coat and figure mean;
Yet still he never threw aside
The pedant's air—the pedant's pride.
Thus, through the streets of this rich place,
He strutted with his usual grace;
And thus he walked about the town,
As if its wealth had been his own:
But of his wealth he could not vapour—
Twelve guineas and a piece of paper
(The present of a noble Lord,)
Was all his pockets did afford:
Though still the lining of his coat
Secreted 'Squire Hearty's note.
And now he thought 'twould not be rash
To turn the paper into cash.
Thus, at his breakfast, while he sat,
And social joined the common chat,

He took occasion to inquire
Who would comply with his desire:
Who would his anxious wish fulfil,
And give him money for his bill.
An arch young sprig, a banker's clerk,
Resolved to hoax the reverend spark
And counselled him to take a range
Among the Merchants on the 'Change.
"Some one, perhaps, may want to send
A payment to a London friend;
He'll in your wishes gladly join,
And take the draft and pay the coin."

The Barber now the Doctor sheared,
And soon whipped off his three-days' beard,
His wig, which had not felt a comb,
Not once since he had quitted home,
Was destined now, with friz and twirl,
To be tormented into curl:
His coat, which had long ta'en the rust,
Was soon deprived of all its dust;
His gaiters too, were fresh japanned;
Such was the Doctor's stern command:
And now with spirits fresh and gay,
To the Exchange he took his way,
To try in this commercial town
A little commerce of his own. [sight;
The Exchange soon met his wondering
The structure filled him with delight.
"Such are the fruits of trading knowledge!
Learning," he cried, "builds no such
college!

Indeed, I entertain a notion,
(I speak the thought with true devotion,)
Though we in Holy Scripture read
That Tyre and Sidon did exceed
In wealth, the cities of the world,
Where ships their wandering sails unfurled,
That e'en her merchants bore the bell
In eating and in drinking well;
Were richer than the lordly great,
And vied with princes in their state;
Yet with all their power and rule,
I think that they ne'er went to school
In such a 'Change as Liverpool."

He entered now—and heard within
The crowded mart—a buzzing din—
A sound confused—the serenade
Of ardent gain, and busy trade:
At length his penetrating eye
Was thrown about him, to descry
Some one in whose sleek, smiling face,
He could the lines of kindness trace;
And soon a person he addressed,
Whose paunch projected from his breast;
Who, looking with good humour fraught,
Appeared the very man he sought;
When, with an unassuming grace,
To him he thus disclosed his case.
"I beg this paper you'll peruse;
And then, perhaps, you'll not refuse

The favour which I ask to grant,
And give the money that I want;
The draft is good—and, on my word,
It was a present from a Lord."

MERCHANT.

"That may be true: but Lords, I fear,
Will meet but little credit here:
'Tis a fair draft upon the view—
Yes! he's a Lord—but who are you?"

SYNTAX.

"Look, and an honest man you'll see,
A Doctor in Divinity,
Whose word's his bond; nor e'er was known
To do a deed he would not own."

MERCHANT.

"I've nought to say—all this may be—
But have you no security?
Pray, Doctor, can't you find a friend
To answer for what you pretend?"

SYNTAX.

"No, I have none!—I am not known
Within the precincts of this town."

MERCHANT.

"And do you come to Liverpool
To find a poor good-natured fool?
With all your learning and your worth,
Pray have you travelled so far north,

To think we have so little wit,
As by such biters to be bit?
To learning we make no pretence.
But, Doctor, we have common sense.
For learned men we do not seek:
And if I may with freedom speak,
I take you for a very Greek."

SYNTAX.

"To know the Greek I do profess—
'Tis my delight and happiness;
And Homer's page I oft have read,
Through the long night, with aching head,
When my wife wanted me in bed."

MERCHANT.

"Then go to Homer, if you will,
And see if he'll discount your bill.
But the clock strikes.—Good bye, old Sinner!
'Tis time for me to go to dinner."

"You want the moneys!" said another,
A bearded, Israelitish brother.
"'Tis a suspected bill, I find;
But you look poor, and I am kind.
Well, we must take the chance of trade;
For twenty pounds the draft is made:
It is too much, as I'm alive,
But give it me—and, here, take five."

"Patience, good Heaven!" the Doctor said;
"Is this the boast and pride of trade!—

Each man they do not know, to treat
As an incorrigible cheat;
And, when he does his want prefer,
To play the base extortioner?
Commerce, I envy not thy gains,
Thy hard-earned wealth, thy golden pains,
(For that's hard-earned, though gained
with ease,
Where Honour's sacred functions cease.)
The dangers which thy votaries run,
Or to undo, or be undone;
Whose hungry maws are daily bent
On the fine feast of cent. per cent.;
Whose virtue, talents, knowledge, health,
Are all combined in that word—wealth.
'Tis a proud scene of moneyed strife
Forms this magnificence of life:
But poor and rich, with all they have,
Will find at length a common grave.
Continue, bounteous Heaven! to me,
A feeling heart, and poverty.
These wights despise me, 'cause I'm poor!
But yet the wretched seek my door:
I fear no Duns, I'm not in debt,
I tremble not at the Gazette:
'Twould to my profit be, and fame,
Did but its page display my name;
Can these proud merchants say the same?"
More he had said—but now his bell
The Beadle rang aloud, to tell
That the good folks should vanish straight,
As he must shut the ponderous gate.

But Syntax did not seem to hear—
So the man rang it in his ear.

SYNTAX.

"I pray, my friend, what's all this rout
With your fierce bell?"

BEADLE.

"To ring you out."

SYNTAX.

"I have been used to hear the din
Of bells that always rang me in."

BEADLE.

"All I've to say, for you to know,
I'll shut the gate if you don't go.
I sure shall leave you in the lurch,
For now, good Sir, you're not at church."

SYNTAX.

"Indeed, my friend, you speak most
true:
I know all that as well as you.
This is no temple; for 'tis clear
I find no money-changers here:
Nor will I say my mind conceives
It may be called a den of thieves.
Howe'er, I'll quit these sons of pelf,
And keep my paper to myself:
They shall no more at Syntax scoff;
Grizzle and I will soon be off.
Thanks to my stars, I've got enough
Of that same yellow, useful stuff,

As will my every want befriend,
And bear me to my journey's end.
Arrived in town, my noble Lord
Will welcome me to bed and board;
When it will make his Lordship sport,
As I these trading tricks report;
How near I was the being cheated;
And how his ancient name was treated."

CANTO XX.

Thus as he spoke, there passed along,
Among the crowding, grinning throng,
One who was in full fashion dressed,
In coat of blue and corded vest,
And seemed superior to the rest.
His small-clothes sat so close and tight;
His boots, like jet, were black and bright,
While the gilt spur, well armed with steel,
Is seen to shine on either heel.
Loaded with seals, and all bespangled,
A watch-chain from his pocket dangled;
His hat a smiling face o'erspread,
And almost hid his well-cropped head:
He swung his whip about to greet
His friends who hurried through the street;
When, as he passed all big with rage,
Syntax appeared upon the stage,
And still continued talking loud
For the amusement of the crowd.

The well-dressed man now stopped, to know
What worked the angry Doctor so;
And, in a pleasant friendly way,
Demanded where his grievance lay:

When, Syntax bowing, on they walked,
And thus the social strangers talked.

SYNTAX.

"These traders, Sir, I can't admire:
You, I presume, Sir, are a 'Squire."

MR. ——.

"I have (and here there passed an oath)
To say the truth, a spice of both:
For now you have within your view
A trader and a 'Squire too.
Here I can some importance claim,
And —— —— is my well-known name,
Nay, there are few within the town
Of more substantial renown.
My house of trade is in this street;
A few miles off my country seat:
Where I most frequently reside
'Mid all the charms of rural pride;—
And I'll be —— if e'er you see
A Lord who better lives than me."

SYNTAX.

"Fie, fie, good Sir, I cannot bear
To hear a fellow-Christian swear;
You must well know such profanation
Is a foul trick in every station;
And will draw down celestial ire
Or on a trader, or a 'Squire:
Nay, 'tis the duty of my cloth,
Whene'er I hear, to check an oath.
I'm a poor Parson—very poor—
I keep a school, and hold a cure;

But when I'm in the parish church,
Or when at home I wield the birch,
I know the dignities that wait
Upon the power of either state:
I keep them always in my view—
Ay, Sir, and I maintain them too.
Nay, in your 'Change, where riches reign,
I did that dignity maintain;
In that proud place, where, I am told,
There sometimes pour down showers of
gold:
But not like that we read of Jove,
For that, you know, was poured for love:
And nothing like it did I see;
Nor love, nor e'en civility:
I only asked a common grace,
When the man mocked me to my face:
Had I an arrant swindler been,
He could not with more scornful mien
Have my polite proposal greeted:
Indeed, I was most foully treated;
And by this dolt was made a joke
Among the rude surrounding folk.
Thus was I worked into a stew,
By Turk, by Gentile, and by Jew:
How bless'd am I to meet with you!
For know, Sir, I've the art to scan
The well-bred, finished gentleman;
And, therefore, I shall lay before you
Some items of my honest story.
The object of the Tour I make
Is chiefly for the profit's sake;

At the same time, I trust, my name
May find some literary fame:
You, if you please, may take a look
At what I've finished of my Book:
A noble Peer doth condescend
To be my patron, and my friend:
I saw him late in York's fair county,
And was the object of his bounty.
This draft, with most becoming grace,
The smile of goodness in his face,
He soft conveyed unto my touch,—
He said, indeed, it was not much;
But could I visit him in town,
He'd make his further friendship known:
And, here, alas! I was so rash
To try to get it changed for cash:
For which, myself and this great Peer,
Of these rude raffs, became the jeer.
Permit me, Sir, to show the paper
That made these purse-proud tradesmen
vapour:
To its full value you'll accord;—
Perhaps, Sir, you may know my Lord."

MR. ———

"I know him well,—'tis his hand-
writing—
It is his Lordship's own inditing:
I'll give the coin:—Why, blood and 'ounds!
I wish 'twere for five hundred pounds!
He is a Lord of great discerning:
His friendship proves your store of learn-
ing;

He's not more known for ancient birth,
Than for the charm of private worth;
For all that elegance and grace
Which decorates a noble race:
Come here with me, and you shall find
At least one trader to your mind."

Syntax now smoothed his angry look,
And straight prepared to show his Book.
In a fine room he soon was seated;
With all attention he was treated;
And while they at their luncheon sat,
Ten minutes passed in friendly chat.
At length the business was arranged;
The deed was done,—the draft was changed;
And, as the Doctor placed his note
In a small pouch within his coat,
"There," said the 'Squire, "there's another:
I've matched it with its very brother,
The Bank of England is their mother;
And when they're offered to her eye,
She'll own them as her progeny.
So tell my Lord, that I for one,
Am proud to do as he has done:
Nor is this all, my learned friend;
Here our acquaintance must not end:
My carriage and my servants wait,
All in due order at the gate:
So you shall go along and see
My rural hospitality.

For a few days we will contrive
To keep our spirits all alive;
I'll send a groom to fetch your mare,
So laugh at thought and banish care."
Thus off they went—and four-in-hand,
Dashed briskly towards the promised
land:
Syntax first told his simple story,
And then the 'Squire detailed his glory.

MR. ———.

"Now we're away in chaise-and-four,
I am a Merchant, Sir, no more,
At least, whene'er I thus retire,
To flourish as a country 'Squire;
And you will see how I prepare
An opiate for mercantile care.
In learned labours some proceed,
But I prefer the racing steed:
Some to Ambition's heights ascend;
I to the Racing-course attend:
In study I ne'er wander far;
Mine is the racing Calendar.
While with keen eye the Heralds see
The long-traced line of ancestry,
Give me a Horse's pedigree.
Others some powerful station boast;
But let me gain the winning post.
It may be sweet with babes to play,
But I prefer the Filly's neigh.
You talk of men of wit and parts,
Of the deep sciences and arts;

Give me the science that will teach
The knowing-one to over-reach:
And, as for pictures and such things,
Which Taste from foreign countries brings;
A brood-mare, in maternal pride,
With a colt trotting by her side,
Is to my eye more pleasing far
Than Hero in triumphant car,
Or sea-born Venus weeping o'er
Adonis, wounded by a boar."

SYNTAX.

"These points, good Sir, I can't discuss;
I know no steed but Pegasus."

MR. ———.

"Cut off his wings,—I've got a horse
Shall run him o'er the Beacon Course;
And, though Apollo should bestride him,
I'll back my horse—for I will ride him."

Thus as he spoke, a row of trees,
Which a full age had felt the breeze,
And half that time, at least, had made
A long cathedral aisle of shade,
Appeared in view, and marked the road
Which led to this brave 'Squire's abode,
Whose stately chambers soon possessed
The Doctor as a welcome guest.
The dinner came—a sumptuous treat;
Nor did the Parson fail to eat
In the same way he used to do—
As much as any other two.

The cakes he munched—the wine he
 quaffed,
His tale he told—the Ladies laughed;
And thus the merry moments passed,
Till cap and slippers came at last.
At length his balmy slumbers o'er,
Morn smiled, as it had smiled before,
And as, without our care or pain,
It will not fail to smile again;
When Syntax, having proved as able
At breakfast, as at dinner table,
Begged leave, with due respect, to say
He must pursue his anxious way.
"No," said the 'Squire, "before you go,
I shall my stud of racers show."
So off they went;—from stall to stall
He showed the steeds, and named them all;
Described their beauty and their birth;
Their well-earned fame and golden worth;
The various feats they all had done,
With plates which they had lost and won.
At length the astonished 'Squire saw
Poor Grizzle to her girths in straw.
"That, Sir," said Syntax, "is my steed;
But though I can't detail her breed,
I sure can tell what she has won—
Those scars by Frenchman's sabre done.
I cannot brag what she has cost;
But you may see what she has lost."
"Where," said the 'Squire, "are her
 ears?"
Quoth Syntax, "you must ask the shears;

And now, perhaps, her switchy tail
Hangs on a barn-door, from a nail!"
The Doctor then began to state
Poor Grizzle's character and fate.
"Who was her dam, or who her sire,
I care not," says the merry 'Squire:
"But well I know, and you shall see,
Who will her noble husband be;
Yon famed gray horse, of Arab birth,
A princely steed, of nameless worth."
"The match is very grand indeed,"
Says Syntax, "but it won't succeed;
Our household is not formed to breed.
My dearest Dorothy and I
Have never had a progeny:
Our fortune has more wisely carved;
Had she borne babes they must have
starved.
What should we do with such dear elves,
Who scarce know how to keep ourselves?"
"I'll hear no more," the 'Squire replied;
"The scheme shall be this moment tried,
Grizzle shall be young Match'em's bride.
You are a very worthy man,
And may the depths of learning scan;
But in these things you're quite a dolt;
You'll get a hundred for the colt.
I'll have my whim—it shall be carried:"—
So Grizzle was that morning married.

And now the 'Squire invites the stay
Of Syntax for another day.

"Your mare," he said, "we'll onward
send
Tied to the London wagon's end:
When she's got forty miles, or more,
We'll follow in a chaise-and-four:
At the Dun Cow, upon the road,
Grizzle shall safely be bestowed;
And there, my friend, or soon or late,
Her master's coming may await:
You'll neither lose nor time nor space—
Your way I'm going to a race,
Where I've a famous horse to run;
And if you do not like the fun,
Why you may then proceed to town,
With my best wishes that renown
And profit may your labours crown.
To-morrow, by the close of day,
We shall find Grizzle on the way."
"Just as you please," the Doctor said;
"Your kind commands shall be obeyed:
I think myself supremely bless'd
By noble minds to be caressed:
The kind protection you impart
Pours oil of gladness on my heart."

The Ladies now desired to see
His journey's pictured history:
The book he showed, which proved a bribe
For those kind fair-ones to subscribe;
And, while they felt the generous pleasure
Of adding to his growing treasure,

The 'Squire, to keep the joke alive,
Had bade his stable folk contrive,
Ere the good Doctor's grizzle mare
Was given to the carrier's care;
Ere on her voyage she set sail,
To furnish her with ears and tail.
Grizzle was soon a crop no more,
As she had been some weeks before;
Nor was it long before her stump
Felt all the honours of the rump:
And thus equipped with specious art,
She paced behind the carrier's cart.
Their breakfast done, the following day,
The 'Squire and Syntax bounced away;
And, ere the sun had set at eve,
The Dun Cow did the sage receive;
Where Grizzle, her day's journey o'er,
Had a short time arrived before.

Syntax now felt a strong desire
To smoke his pipe by kitchen fire,
Where many a country neighbour sat,
Nor did he fail to join the chat;
When, having supped and drank his ale,
And silence seeming to prevail,
He slowly from his pocket took
His travelling memorandum book;
And, as he turned the pages o'er,
Revolving on their curious lore,
The exciseman, a right village sage,
(For he could cast accounts and gauge,)

Spoke for the rest—who would be proud
To hear his Reverence read aloud.
He bowed assent, and straight began
To state what beauty is in man;
Or on the surface of the earth,
Or what finds, in its entrails, birth:
With all things in their due degrees,
That live in air or love the seas;
In all the trees and plants that grow,
In all the various flowers that blow;
Of all things in the realms of nature,
Of senseless forms, or living creature:
In short he thus professed to show,
Through all the vast expanse below,
From what concentred state of things
The varying form of beauty springs.
But, as he read, though full of grace,
Though strong expression marked his face,
Though his feet struck the sounding floor,
And his voice thundered through the door,
Each hearer as the infection crept
O'er his numbed sense, unconscious slept!
One dropped his pipe—another snored,
His bed of down an oaken board:
The cobbler yawned, then sunk to rest,
His chin reclining on his breast:
All slept at length but Tom and Sue,
For they had something else to do.
Syntax heard naught; the enraptured elf
Saw and heard nothing but himself:
But, when a swineherd's bugle sounded,
The Doctor then, amazed—confounded,

Beheld the death-like scene about him;
And, thinking it was formed to flout him,
He frowned disdain—then struck his head,
Caught up a light, and rushed to bed.

CANTO XXI.

Sleep, to the virtuous ever kind,
Soon hushed the Doctor's turbid mind,
And, when the morning shed its dew,
He rose his journey to pursue.
Of tea and toast he took his fill,
Then told the Host to bring the bill;
But when it came, it made him stare
To see some curious items there.
"Go tell your Ostler to appear;
I wish to see the fellow here."
The Ostler now before him stands,
And bows his head, and rubs his hands.—
"In this same bill, my friend, I see
You're witty on my mare and me:
For all your corn, and beans, and hay,
'Tis a fair charge which I shall pay:
But here a strange demand appears—
'For cleaning of her tail and ears!'
Now know, my lad, if this be done
On me to play your vulgar fun,
(For ears and tail my mare has none,)
I'll make this angry horse-whip crack
In all directions on your back."
The man denied all ill intent;
He knew not what his Reverence meant:

So thought it best to say no more,
But bring up Grizzle to the door.
Of painted canvas were her ears;
Upon her stump a tail appears;
So changed she was, so gay, so smart,
Decked out with so much curious art,
That even Syntax hardly dare
To claim his metamorphosed mare.
He said no more—he knew the joke
Was not the sport of vulgar folk;
So trotted off—and kindly lent
His smile to aid the merriment.

Now, as his journey he pursued,
He thus broke forth in solemn mood:—
"Though time draws on when those at home
Expect that I should cease to roam,
(Though I have objects in my view
Which are of great importance too,)
Yet, as this is the day of rest
Appointed both for man and beast,
To the first church I will repair,
And pay my solemn duties there."

Thus as he spoke, a village chime
Denoted it was service time:
And soon a ruddy Curate came,
To whom he gravely told his name,
His rank, and literary fame;
And said, as he'd been used to teaching,
He'd give him half an hour's preaching.

This was accepted with a smile,
And they both strutted up the aisle;
When, in due time, and with due grace,
Syntax displayed his preaching face.
And in bold tones, though somewhat
hoarse,
He gave the following discourse:—

"The subject I shall now rehearse,
Is Job the fifth,—the seventh verse:—
"'As sparks rise upwards to the sky,
So man is born to misery.'

"This is a truth we all can tell;
In every state we know it well:
The infant in his cradle lies,
And marks his trouble as he cries:
From his young eyes the waters flow,
The emblems of his future woe:
His cheeks the varying scenes display
That mark a changeful April day:
Symbols of joy and hope appear,
And now a smile, and then a tear.
The years of puling childhood o'er,
The nurse's care he knows no more:
To Learning's discipline resigned,
The Tutor forms his early mind;
And hopes and fears alternate rise,
In all their strange varieties.
How oft, disdainful of restraint,
His voice lifts up the loud complaint,
While stern correction's powerful law
Keeps the young urchin-mind in awe,

And some dark cloud for ever lowers,
To shade his bright and playful hours.
Nor, when fair Reason's steady ray
Begins to light Life's early day;
Though the thick mist it instant clears,
It dries not up the source of tears;
Nay, 'tis its office, as we know,
Sometimes to make those tears to flow.
For now the Passions will impart
Their impulse to the unconscious heart;
Will mingle in Youth's ardent hours,
And plant the thorns amid the flowers;
While Fancy, in its various guise,
With plumage of a thousand dyes,
Flits round the mind in wanton play,
To bear each serious thought away.
The Pleasures seldom tempt in vain
To join their gay, deluding train;
Courting the easy hearts to stray
From Reason's path, and Wisdom's way.
And oh! how oft the senses cloy
With what is called the height of Joy!
While pale Repentance comes at last,
To execrate the Pleasure past!
—At length to finished manhood grown,
The world receives him as its own.
Life's active busy scenes engage
Each moment of maturer age:
Here Pleasure courts him to her bowers,
Where serpents lurk beneath the flowers.

—Ambition tempts him to explore
The height where daring spirits soar,
While Wealth presents the glittering ore,
Which mingles in each mortal plan,
And is the great concern of man.
—Thus Pleasure, Wealth, or love of
power,
Employ man's short or lengthened hour.
"In youth or manhood's early day,
Pleasure first meets him on the way.
The Syren sings, his eager ear
Drinks in the sound so sweet to hear;
To the delicious song a slave,
He leaves his vessel to the wave:
The helm forsaken, on it goes,
The lightnings flash, the whirlwind blows:
When, by the furious tempest tossed,
The gay, the gilded, bark is lost!
But should he, 'mid the ocean's roar,
Be cast upon some distant shore;
Then, wandering on the lonely coast,
He sighs to think what he has lost;
Health, ease, and every joy that Heaven
Had to his early wishes given.
Life still is his—but Life alone
Cannot for follies past atone,
When Pain assails, and Hope is flown.
He feels no more the sunny rays
Of smiling hours and prosperous days:
The world turns from him, nor will know
The man of sorrow and of woe;

But bids him to some cell repair,
In hope to find Contrition there.
"Nor is Ambition more secure,
Nor less the ills which they endure
Within whose breast is seen to dwell
The vice by which the Angels fell.
The love of rule, the thirst of power,
Ne'er give a peaceful, tranquil hour;
'Tis the fierce fever of the soul
That maddens for supreme control;
Whose burning thirst continual grows;
Whose pride no lasting pleasure knows:
While Hatred, Envy, jealous Fear,
Wait on the proud and bold career.
Contention every act attends;
Now friends are foes—now foes are friends:
Enjoyment quickens new desire,
And Hope for ever fans the fire.
Whene'er the nearer height is gained,
A loftier still must be attained;
And then the eye looks keenly round
In hope another's to be found;
One—such is the aspiring soul—
Whose towering height shall crown the whole.
But oft as the aspirant gains
The object of his toil and pains,
The giddy view each sense appals—
In vain for some kind help he calls;
The faithless friend, the insulting foe,
Rejoice as to the gulph below

He headlong falls—a prey to lie
Of grinning Scorn and Infamy.
"Now riches next demand our thought:
But gold may be too dearly bought,
As in each clime and every soil,
It wakes the universal toil.
For this, defying health and ease,
The Sailor ploughs the distant seas;
This shares the daring Soldier's aim,
Who fights for wealth as well as fame:
But, though all wish its power to wear,
It is the source of many a care.
—Of all the vices that infest
The purlieus of the human breast,
The love of Mammon is the worst,
The most detested and accurst.
Pleasure's gay moments may impart
Some gladness to the human heart;
Ambition, too, we often find
The inmate of a noble mind;
But love of riches ever bears
The token of the lowest cares.
We see one base unvarying vice
In the pale form of Avarice:
It only lifts its prayer to Heaven
To increase the store already given;
Nor does it e'er the gift repay,
By shedding one kind cheering ray
Upon the weather-beaten shed,
Where Want scarce finds the scanty bread,
By wiping from the widow's eye
The flowing tears of misery;

Or giving to the naked form
The vestment that will keep it warm.
For gold it courts the sleepless night,
And toils through day's returning light:
Nor these alone;—the cool deceit—
The treacherous heart—the hidden cheat—
The ready lie—the hard demand—
And Law's oppressive griping hand;
These demons never fail to wait
At Mammon's dark and dreary gate.
What does he love! can it be told?
Yes, I can tell:—he loves his gold:
In that one term he comprehends
His kindred, neighbourhood, and friends.
But e'en should Fortune daily pour
Her treasures to increase his store,
Say, is he happy?—Does he feel
A pleasure which he dare reveal?
Ah, no!—his throbbing anxious breast
Continued doubts and fears molest.
See how he trembles with affright
When Justice claims the widow's right,
And bids him at the bar appear,
To answer to the Orphan's tear,
By restoration to atone
For many a wrong that he has done.
Nay, a still far severer doom
May aggravate the time to come:
The scourge without, the scourge within,
May lash the unavailing sin;

And, after all his toil and care,
'Tis well if he escape Despair.
"But e'en when Pleasure is not crossed
With ruined health and fortune lost,
Yet still it leaves a void behind—
And dulness stupifies the mind.
The season of enjoyment o'er,
The phantom then can please no more:
Brief is its time, it soon is past:
A vernal bloom not made to last.
Say, what presents its longest doom?
A flower, a fever, and a tomb!
"What though Ambition holds its power
To Life's extreme, but certain hour,
Is not its most exalted joy
Encumbered with some base alloy?
And, on its proudest, loftiest height,
Say, does it always find delight?
Say, could it ever guard its heart
From Fear's assault, and Envy's dart?
It cannot shut the averted eye
From passing life's mortality.
E'en from its most aspiring brow,
It must behold a grave below.
"Though Wealth should haply be attained
By fair pursuits, with honour gained,
Yet in its train how oft we see
The pallid forms of misery.
Intemperance yields its foul delight,
And feeds the obnoxious appetite;

While Luxury in a thousand ways
To sensual carelessness betrays,
And lights up in the mortal frame
Disease's slow corroding flame.
Fortune, in fickle mood, may frown;
The firmest base may tumble down:
While it appears in strength secure,
It falls and leaves its owner poor.
The largest heaps of treasured wealth
Cannot restore declining health;
They cannot bribe the sun to stay,
And mitigate his burning ray;
Nor will the North's imperious cold
Dissolve to genial warmth for gold.
Time will not one short moment stay,
Though millions lay athwart his way;
Nor all the wealth that Crœsus bore
Can add to Life one moment more.
The regal palace and the cot
Are subject to one common lot:
The rich and poor, the small and great,
Alike must feel the stroke of fate:
Virtue alone, we ought to know,
Is real happiness below;
And yet how oft her kindness proves,
By pain and toil, the child she loves.
Honour, of noble minds the flower,
Is oft betrayed by Treachery's power:
And Charity, we often see,
The dupe of base Hypocrisy.
"Who then will venture to declare
That man's mistitled sorrow's heir?

But, Brethren, let us not complain,
That Heaven's unjust when we sustain
The allotted term of Care and Pain.
Our life in such a mould is cast,
'Tis plain it is not made to last:
'Tis but a state of trial here,
To fit us for a purer sphere;
A scene of contest for a prize
That in another region lies;
In better worlds and brighter skies:
Here doomed a painful lot to bear,
Our Happiness is treasured there.
To struggle with the woes of life,
To wage with evil constant strife;
To oppose the Passions as they rise,
And check their wild propensities;
To improve our nature, and to bear
With patience, the allotted share
Of human woes—and thus fulfil
The wise and the eternal will,
That forms the grand, mysterious plan
For Mortal and Immortal man.
"Man is, indeed, by Heaven's decree,
As happy as he ought to be;
As suited to his state and nature,
A restless, frail, and finite creature:
His work well done—his labour o'er—
Evil and sorrow are no more;
And, having passed the vale of death,
He claims the never-fading wreath;
Glory's Eternal Crown to share,
Which Cherubs sing, and Angels wear:

Then is complete the amazing plan,
And Mortal is Immortal man."

Here Syntax thought it fit to close:—
The admiring congregation rose;
And after certain hems and ha's,
The 'Squire nodded his applause:
Nay, such attention he had given
To the sage Minister of Heaven,
That neither did he sleep nor snore—
A wonder never known before.
Then quickly issuing from his pew,
He came to thank the Doctor too.
"Sir, your discourse so good and fine,
Proves you to be a great Divine,
While I, alas! am but a sinner;
So you'll go home with me to dinner;
And, shortly after evening prayer,
The Curate too, will meet you there."
The Doctor found the house well stored:
A chattering wife, and plenteous board:
The dinner was a pleasing sight,
For preaching gets an appetite;
And Syntax could perform them both
As well as any of the cloth.
At length, the eatables removed,
The 'Squire began the talk he loved.

'SQUIRE.

"Have you much game, Sir, where you live?"

SYNTAX.

"An answer, Sir, I scarce can give:
I never hunt, nor bear a gun;
I have no time, nor like the fun.
Learning's the game which I pursue:
I have no other sport in view:
But I have heard—the country round
With hares and partridge does abound;
Though on my table it is rare
To see or one or t'other there.
Oft when I rise at early morn,
And hear the cheerful, echoing horn,
I'm forced from the inspiring noise,
To hunt a pack of idle boys;
And when they babble, in their din,
I am a special whipper-in:
Nay, if they should be found at fault,
I crack my whip, Sir, as I ought."

Syntax now told his story o'er,
A story told so oft before;
When soon the 'Squire began to feel
A slumber o'er his senses steal:
The Curate, too, bemused in beer,
Was more disposed to sleep than hear.
Says Syntax, "See the effect of drink!
Heaven spare the souls which cannot think!
But I will not their sleep molest;
The Sabbath is a day of rest."

In short, his words no more prevail;
There now were none to hear his tale:
He strove another pipe to smoke,
But there were none to hear his joke:
So on his elbow he reclined,
And thus the sleeping party joined.
—The clock struck ten ere they awoke;
When a shrill voice their slumbers broke:
In such a tone it seemed to come,
That Syntax thought himself at home.
So, having yawned and shook their heads,
They wished good-night, and sought their
beds.

CANTO XXII.

THE clock struck five when Syntax woke;
The sounding door his slumbers broke:
When a soft female voice related
That breakfast and her master waited:
Up rose the Doctor, down he went,
With joyful look and heart content.
"Well," said the 'Squire, "I hope you'll
stay
And pass with me another day;
The sporting season's coming on,
And something now is to be done:
For I must breathe my dogs a-bit,
And try my gun at some tom-tit.
You'll take a stroll around the fields,
And see what game my manor yields."
Says Syntax, "'Tis not in my power
To pass with you another hour;
While you perform your sporting feats,
I must be tramping London streets:
You, therefore, will my thanks receive,
For now, Sir, I must take my leave."
The 'Squire replied—"All I can say—
Another time a longer stay."
He then walked off with dog and gun,
While Syntax travelled slowly on;

And, o'er the hill, or on the plain,
Indulged the contemplative strain.

"I cannot, while I Nature view,
Clothed in her robe of verdant hue,
Or when the changeful veil is thrown,
Of Summer's gold or Autumn's brown,
Or midst the scenes of snow and frost,
When her gay colouring is lost;
I cannot but the Power admire
That gives such charms to her attire:
Nor do her wondrous shapes, that rise
In countless forms to meet the eyes,
Mark with less force the unerring soul,
Which with such beauty decks the whole.
The mountain's top that seems to meet
The height of Heaven's Imperial seat;
The rocks, the valley's guardian pride,
Or boundaries of the ocean's tide,
That oft, in grand confusion hurled,
Seem like the fragments of a world;
While the low hill and vale between,
Appear to variegate the scene.
But lesser forms invite to trace
Fair Nature's ever-varying face:
The humble shrub, the spreading tree,
In this same principle agree.
Along the ground the brambles crawl,
And the low hyssop tops the wall;
The bulrush rises from the sedge,
The wild-rose blossoms in the hedge;

While flowers of every colour shed
A fragrance from their native bed.
The streamlet, winding through the glade,
The hanging wood, the forest shade;
The river's bold and flowing wave,
Doth many a peopled margin lave,
Till, with increasing course, 'tis seen
To blend its white waves with the green.
Nor these alone;—how various they
Who cleave the air, or skim the sea,
Or range the plain, or from the brow,
Look down upon the vale below:
The cygnet's snow, the peacock's dyes,
The pigeon's neck, the eagle's eyes;
Nor in less beauty do they rove,
Who form the music of the grove.
The elephant's resistless force;
The strength and spirit of the horse;
The ermine's softness, and the boar,
With rising bristles covered o'er.
Thus throughout Nature's various state,
Of living or inanimate,
In every different class we see
How boundless the variety!
What playful change in all we know
Of this mysterious world below;
In all where instinct motion gives,
In what by vegetation lives:
But these are trivial when we look
Through the first page of Nature's book,
When, half-inspired, we're taught to scan
The vast varieties of man."

Thus, in deep metaphysic mood,
Syntax his shortened way pursued:
And many a system had been brought
To ripen in his learned thought;
But none arose which did not tend
Poor human nature to befriend;
None but were aptly formed to prove
The firm support of social love.
Thus, all bemused he took his way,
Unconscious of the passing day;
And, thus employed in cogitating,
No wonder he ne'er thought of baiting;
No wonder that it came to pass
When Grizzle saw a little grass,
That he, contemplating the view
Of knotty questions, never knew
She stopped to take a bite or two;
Or, when they passed a limpid brook,
That she a plenteous beverage took;
Or if, by chance upon the road,
They found a cart with hay well stowed,
She lagged behind to crop the fare,
And levy contributions there.

But now a Trumpet's warlike sound
Woke Syntax from his dream profound;
While Grizzle frisked, and moved on straight
With many a prancing to the gate,
Where, in a gorgeous cap of fur,
Stood the proclaiming Trumpeter,

With face as the old Lion red,
Which dangling hung above his head.
"Oh!" he exclaimed, "I now could swear
I see again the Grizzle mare;
I know her well by that same scar
Which she got with me in the war:
For she received that angry hack
When I was sounding on her back;
A furious Hussar onward came,
And struck at me but missed his aim;
When my poor mare received the blow,
And straight the blood began to flow;
Nay, the same sword had cracked my
    crown,
But my brave comrade Stephen Brown
Came up and cut the Frenchman down.
I have been borne by that same gray
Through many a rough and bloody day:
Her ears well know the martial strain;—
I'm glad to see her once again."

"That well may be;—but for her ears—
A wicked clown's infernal shears
Have robbed her," Syntax smiling said,
"Of the fair honours of her head;
Nor did one tender thought prevail,
From the same fate to save her tail."
He then proceeded to relate
Her past mishap and present state;
And asked the Trumpeter to share
A flowing bowl and evening fare.

Now Syntax sat and heard the story
The soldier told of England's glory;
How British columns fought their way,
And drove the foe, and won the day:
How oft did he his breath enlarge,
To call to arms and sound the charge;
But, though he roused to many a feat,
He never sounded a retreat.
Still he declaimed in modest tone—
For England's glory was his own.

"Oft have I seen in bright array,
(Sure promise of a glorious day)
The martial bands alive to meet
Their foes, and lay them at their feet;
And, when my breathing trumpet told 'em
To go and conquer—to behold 'em,
At once their beaming blades display,
And rush on their victorious way,
I felt the inexpressive joy
Which grim-faced danger could not cloy.
If that same grizzle steed you rode
Could speak, she'd tell the ground she trod
Was oft, alas! all covered o'er
With soldiers slain and clotted gore.
Full many a hair-breadth 'scape I've seen;
In many a peril I have been;
And soon again the time may come,
When, ordered from our native home,
We shall seek foreign climes to share
The dangers and the din of war.

So be it, I'm prepared to go,
Wherever I may meet the foe;
And should it be my lot to die,
I have no wife or babes to cry;
And 'mid what bloodshed I may fall,
There'll be an end of Thomas Hall."

Said Syntax, "It is well, my friend,
To be prepared to meet our end:
To do that well, I'm called to preach;
'Tis a prime duty which I teach;
But thoughts of a far different kind
Just now employ my anxious mind:
The present busy hours must claim
Attention to my purse and fame;
And, as I think 'twould prove a joke
To show my mare to London folk,
It has just come into my mind
To leave poor Grizzle here behind,
And let some stage or mail convey
My bags and me my onward way.
Perhaps, for old-acquaintance sake,
Of my poor beast the care you'll take."
"If so,"—the Trumpeter replied—
"'Twill be my honour and my pride.
God bless your Reverence,—never fear—
Your mare shall have protection here:
When you return her looks will tell,
That her Old Friend has used her well."

A horn now told the near approach
Of some convenient, rapid coach;

And soon a vehicle and four
Appeared at the Red Lion door:
Into his place the Doctor pounced;
The coachman smacked, and off they
bounced.
The scene around was quite composing,
For his companions all were dozing;
So he, forsooth, conceived it best
To close his lids and try to rest.
When the morn dawned he turned an eye
Upon his slumbering company:
A red-faced man, who snored and snorted,
A lady, with both eyes distorted,
And a young miss of pleasing mien,
With all the life of gay sixteen.
A sudden jolt their slumbers broke;
They started all, and all awoke;
When Surly-boots yawned wide, and
spoke:—
"We move," said he, "confounded slow:"
"La, Sir," cried Miss, "How fast we go!"
While Madam, with a smirking face,
Declared it was a middling pace.
"Pray, what think you, Sir?"—"I agree,"
Said simpering Syntax, "with all three:
Up hill, our course is rather slow;
Down hill, how merrily we go!
But, when 'tis neither up nor down,
It is a middling pace I own."
"O la!" cried miss, "the thought's so
pretty!"
"O yes!" growled Red-face, "very witty!"

The lady said, "If I can scan
The temper of the gentleman,
He's one of those, I have no doubt,
Who loves to let his humour out:
Nor fails his thread-bare wit to play
On all who come within his way:
But we who in these stages roam,
And leave our coach-and-four at home,
Deserve our lot when thus we talk
With those who were ordained to walk!
And now, my niece, you see how wrong
It is to use your flippant tongue,
And chatter as you're apt to do
With any one—the Lord knows who."
Surly turned round, and friendly sleep
Soon o'er his senses 'gan to creep!
So Syntax thought he'd overlook
The embryo of his future Book;
Thus all was silence till they came
To the great town we London name.

Our sage thought wisely that the din
Which he should hear about an Inn,
Would not assist his studious hours,
Nor aid his intellectual powers
To make his volume fit to show
The Dons of Paternoster Row;
And as his Patron of the North,
That Lord renowned for sense and worth,
Had bid him make his house his home
Whenever he to town should come,

He was resolved to try his fate
In knocking at his Lordship's gate.
At that same gate he soon appeared;
My Lord with smiles the Doctor cheered.
"You have done well, my learned friend,
Hither your early steps to bend;
Business has brought me up to town,
And thus you find me all alone:
Here pitch your tent, and pass your hour
In working up your pleasant Tour;
And when 'tis done, I'll aid your scheme—
It shall not prove an idle dream."
Syntax received his Lordship's grace
With moistened eye, but smiling face,
And for ten days, at morn and night,
He toiled to bring his book to light;
While the few intervening hours
Were rendered gay with wine and flowers.*

My Lord, by generous friendship moved,
Now read his volume, and approved.
"Think not," said he, "I fondly give
Opinions, tending to deceive:
That I'm sincere, my friend, you'll see,
When I declare that you are free
To dedicate your book to me;
Nor is this all—I'll recommend
My very pleasant, learned friend

---

* Huc vina et unguenta et nimium breves,
Flores amœnæ ferre jube rosæ.

Hor.

To one who has as liberal feeling
As any in this kind of dealing:
And when my letter you present,
He'll take the work, and give content.
Thus, my good Sir, I've done my best:
You'll see him, and explain the rest."

The Doctor now received his papers
In spirits almost to cut capers;
Nor did he then delay to go,
Not to the realms of sight and show,
But those of Paternoster Row.
The shop he entered;—all around
He saw the shelves with volumes crowned,
In Russia and Morocco bound:
And when he had, with fond delight,
Glanced o'er the literary sight,
"Go, call you master," Syntax said
To an attendant on the trade;
"Tell him that a D. D. is here:"
The lad then answered, with a sneer,
"To no D. D. will he appear;
He would not come for all the knowledge
Of Oxford or of Cambridge College:
I cannot go, as I'm a sinner;
I dare not interrupt his dinner:
You know not how I should be blamed."
Stamping his foot, Syntax exclaimed,
"Apollo and the Muses nine!
Must Learning wait while Tradesmen
dine?"

"They're common hacks," replied the boy:
"We never such as those employ;
I've heard their names, but this I know,
They seldom come into the Row."
The master, who had filled his crop
In a smart room behind the shop,
On hearing a loud angry voice,
Came forth to know what caused the noise;
And left his wife and bottle too,
To see about this strange to-do.
He was a man whose ample paunch
Was made of beef, and ham, and haunch:
And when he saw the shrivelled form
Of Syntax, he began to storm.

BOOKSELLER.

"I wish to know, Sir, what you mean,
By kicking up, Sir, such a scene?
And who you are, Sir, and your name,
And on what errand here you came?"

SYNTAX.

"My errand was to bid you look
With care and candour on this Book;
And tell me whether you think fit
To buy, or print, or publish it?
The subject which the work contains
Is Art and Nature's fair domains;
'Tis formed the curious to allure;—
In short, good man, it is a Tour;
With Drawings all from Nature made,
And with no common skill displayed:

Each house, each place, each lake, each
tree,
These fingers drew—these eyes did see."

BOOKSELLER.

"A Tour, indeed! I've had enough
Of Tours, and such-like flimsy stuff.
What a fool's errand you have made,
(I speak the language of the trade,)
To travel all the country o'er,
And write what has been writ before!
We can get Tours—don't make wry faces,
From those who never saw the places.
I know a man who has the skill
To make you Books of Tours at will;
And from his garret in Moorfields
Can see what every country yields;
So, if you please, you may retire,
And throw your Book into the fire:
You need not grin, my friend, nor vapour;
I would not buy it for waste paper."

SYNTAX.

"Blockhead! and is it thus you treat
The men by whom you drink and eat?
Do you not know, and must I tell ye,
'Tis they fill out your monstrous belly?
Yes, booby! from such skulls as mine
You lap your soup, and drink your wine,
Without one single ray of sense
But what relates to pounds and pence.
Thus good and evil form the whole—
Heaven gave you wealth, and me a soul:

And I would never be an ass
For all your gold, with all your brass.
When humble Authors come to sue,
(Those very men that pamper you,)
You feel like Jove in all his pride,
With Juno squatting by his side."

BOOKSELLER.

"How dare you, villain, to defame
My dearest wife's unsullied name?
Yes, she's my wife! ten years ago
The Parson joined our hands at Bow,
And she's the flower of all our Row.
As for Miss Juno, she's a harlot,
You foul-mouthed, and malicious varlet!
A prostitute, who is well known
To all the rakes about the town;
First with a footman off she ran,
And now lives with an Alderman."

SYNTAX.

"Have done—have done! pray read that letter,
And then I think you'll treat me better."

BOOKSELLER.

"Sir, had you shown the letter first,
My very belly should have burst
Before I would have said a word
Your learned ears should not have heard;
But, in this world wherein we live,
We must forget, Sir, and forgive.

These little heats will sometimes start
From the most friendly, generous heart.
My Lord speaks highly of your merit,
As of the talents you inherit;
He writes himself supremely well;
His works are charming—for they sell.
I pray you take a glass of wine;
Perhaps, Sir, you have yet to dine:
We now, I fear, have nothing hot:
My dear, put something in the pot;
'Twill soon be done; or tell our Nan
To toss a cutlet in the pan.
His Lordship here expressly says
Your work transcends his utmost praise;
Desires the printing may commence,
And he'll be bound for the expense.
The Book will sell, I have no doubt,
I'll spare no pains to bring it out:
A work like this must not be stinted,
Two thousand copies shall be printed.
And if you please—"

SYNTAX.

"I cannot stay;
We'll talk of that another day;
When I came out, I gave my word
To take my dinner with my Lord."

BOOKSELLER.

"Perhaps some other time you'll come,
When my good Lord may dine from home;
It will be kind indeed, to share,
Quite as a friend, our humble fare;

In the mean time you may command,
In every sense, my heart and hand."

Thus (such are this world's odds and ends)
Though foes they met—they parted friends.

CANTO XXIII.

"Whate'er of genius or of merit
The child of labour may inherit,
They will not, in this mortal state,
Or give him wealth, or make him great,
Unless that strange capricious dame,
Whom Pagan poets Fortune name,
That unseen, ever active power,
Propitious, aids his toilsome hour.
Throughout my life I've struggled hard;
And what has been my lean reward?
What have I gained by learned lore,
By deeply reading o'er and o'er,
What every ancient sage has writ;
Renowned for pure and Attic wit;
Or those rich volumes which dispense
The strains of Roman eloquence?
No favouring patrons have I got,
But just enough to boil the pot.
What though by toil and pain, I know
Where every Hebrew root doth grow,
And can each hidden truth descry
From Genesis to Malachi;
Yet I have never been decreed
To shear the fleeces that I feed:
No, they enrich the idle dunce
Who never saw his flock but once,

And meanly grudges e'en to spare
My pittance for their weekly fare.
Have I made any real friends,
By wasting eyes and candles' ends?
And though a good musician too,
What did my fiddle ever do?
I sometimes might employ its powe,
To soothe an over-anxious hour:
But though it with my temper suits,
It never yet could soften brutes.
My sketching-pencil, too, is known
In every house throughout the town;
For, to replace some horrid scrawl,
My drawings hang on every wall:
And yet, 'tis true, as I'm a sinner,
They seldom paid me with a dinner.
What do I get poor boys to teach?
And drive in learning at the breech?
A task, which Lucian says, is given
As the worst punishment from Heaven.
While Fortune's boobies cut and carve,
I may be said to teach and starve;
Too happy, if on Chrismas-day,
I've just enough the duns to pay.
Though sometimes I have almost swore,
When from the threshold of the door,
My poverty repelled the poor;
When the cask, emptied of its ale,
No more the thirsty could regale.

"At length the lucky moment came
To fill my purse and give me fame;

And, after all my labours past,
Hope bids me look for rest at last.
For scarce had I one prosperous hour
Till Fortune bid me Write a Tour.
Oft have I said in words unkind,
That strumpet Fortune's very blind!
But now I think the wench can see,
Since she's become so kind to me.
To say the truth, I scarce believe
The favours which I now receive:
In a Lord's house I take my rest,
A welcome and an honoured guest:
The favours on my Tour I found
Are by his present kindness crowned.
I'd always heard that these same Lords
Were only friendly in their words:
Truth can alone my patron move,
Whose generous deeds his promise prove."

Thus Syntax did his feelings broach,
As he reclined within a coach:
For, pondering as he passed along,
He was sore pummelled by the throng:
Now by a porter's package greeted,
Now on the pavement he was seated;
While, deafened by a news-boy's din,
A fruit-girl's barrow strikes his shin;
And as his cautious course he guides,
The passing elbows punch his sides:
While a cart-wheel, with luckless spirt,
Gives him a taste of London dirt:

At length, to get in safety back,
He sought the comforts of a Hack.

His little journey at an end,
The Doctor joined his noble friend:
Together they in comfort dine,
Then munched their cakes, and sipped
their wine;
When Syntax, briefly, thus displayed
His parley with the man of trade:—

"I owe unto your Lordship's name
My future gains in gold and fame.
My uncombed wig,—my suit of black,
Which had grown rusty on my back,
My grizly visage, pale and thin,
My carcase, nought but bones and skin,
Presented to the Tradesman's eye
The ghastly form of Poverty:
Nor would he deign to cast a look
Upon the pages of my book;
But, with the fierceness of a Turk,
In sorry terms reviled my work;
And let loose all his purse-proud spleen
Against a thing he ne'er had seen.
But your kind note, where it was said
That all expenses should be paid,
New-dyed my coat, new-cocked my hat,
Powdered my wig, and made me fat.
His eye now saw me plump and sleek,
With not a wrinkle on my cheek;

And strength, and stateliness, and vigour
Completed my important figure;
While, in my pocket, his keen look
Glanced at your Lordship's pocket-book.
'Twas now—'I'm sure the work will sell,
And pay the learned author well:'
Then graced his shrill and sputtering
speeches
With pulling up his monstrous breeches;
And made me all the humblest bows
His vast protuberance allows:
For had he come with purse in hand,
E'en Satan might his press command;
So that the book had not a flaw
To risk the dangers of the law.
Prove but his gains, and he'd be civil,
Or to the Doctor or the Devil."

Thus Syntax and his patron sat,
And thus prolonged the evening chat.

MY LORD.

"Your rapid pencil fairly traces
Men's characters as well as faces.
Your latter sketch is true to Nature,
And gives me Vellum's every feature.
With all your various talents fraught,
So deeply read, so ably taught,
I feel a curious wish to know
From whence your high endowments flow:
And how it happens that a man,
Whose worth I scarce know how to scan,

Should ne'er have reached a better state,
Than seems to be your present fate."

SYNTAX.

"My Lord, a very scanty page
Will tell my birth and parentage:
A moderate circle will contain
My round of pleasure and of pain,
Till you, my ever-honoured friend,
Bade my horizon wide extend,
And lighted up a brighter ray
To beam upon my clouded day.

"My father was a noble creature
As e'er was formed by pregnant Nature;
A learned Clerk, a sound Divine,
A favorite of the Virgins nine
Who dwell upon Parnassian hill,
Or bathe in Heliconian rill.
In the sequestered vale of life,
An equal foe to pride and strife,
He passed his inoffensive day
In teaching Virtue's peaceful way:
A shepherd, formed his flock to bless
In this world's thorny wilderness,
And lead them, when their time is o'er,
To where, good man, he's gone before.
Ambition ne'er disturbed his rest,
Nor bred a serpent in his breast
To sting his peace: no sordid care
Corroded the contentment there:
While he possessed an income clear
Of full five hundred pounds a year.

"My mother, first of woman-kind,
In figure, feature, and in mind,
In her calm sphere contented moved,
The counterpart of him she loved.
Formed to adorn the highest lot,
She graced the Vicar's rural cot,
With all those manners that became
The Parson's wife, the village dame.
They lived and loved—and might have
wore
The Flitch, when twenty years were o'er.

"An only child appeared to prove
The pledge of fond, connubial love.
I was that child—a darling boy;
Their daily hope—their daily joy.
My anxious father did not spare
The urchin to another's care;
He taught the little forward elf
To be the image of himself;
And from the cradle he began
To form and shape the future man.
When fifteen summer suns had shed
Their lustre on my curly head,
To *Alma Mater* he consigned,
With pious hope, my ripening mind.

"There, seven short years (tor short
they were)
Fair science was my only care;
I gave my nights, I gave my days,
To Tully's page, and Homer's lays.

Whate'er is known of ancient lore
I fondly studied o'er and o'er:
I followed each appointed course,
And traced up learning to its source,
But in my way I gathered flowers;
I sought the Muses in their bowers,
And did their favouring smiles repay
With many a lyric roundelay;
Nor did I fail the arts to woo
Of Music and of Painting too.
Thus was my early manhood passed
In happiness too great to last.
My father died—and ere his urn
Had filled my arms, I had to mourn
A mother, who refused to stay,
When her loved mate was ta'en away.

"What followed?—I was left alone,
And the world seized me as its own.
I sought gay Fashion's motley throng,
On Pleasure's tide I sailed along;
Till, by rude storms and tempests tossed,
My shattered bark at length was lost,
While I stood naked on the shore,
My treasure gone, my pleasure o'er.

"Now changed by Fortune's fickle wind,
The friends I cherished proved unkind:
All those who shared my prosperous day,
Whene'er they saw me—turned away:
And, as I almost wanted bread,
I undertook a bear to lead,

To see the brute perform his dance,
Through Holland, Italy, and France:
But it was such a very Bruin,
To be with him was worse than ruin;
So, having paced o'er classic ground,
And sailed the Grecian Isles around,
(A pleasure, sure, beyond compare,
Though linked in couples with a bear,)
I took my leave, and left the cub
Some humble Swiss to pay and drub.
Yet, when I reached my native shore,
Determined to lead bears no more,
No better prospect did I see,
Than a free-school and curacy;
The country tradesmen's sons to teach;
In lonely village-church to preach,
With the proud sneer and vulgar taunt,
Oft thrown at Learning when in want;
All which you'll think, my noble friend,
Did not to ease or comfort tend.
But now, another act displays
The folly of my former days:
A new scene opens of my life;
For faith, my Lord, I took a wife."

MY LORD.

"I should have thought a married mate
Must have improved your lonely state!
That a kind look and winning smile
Would serve your labours to beguile."

SYNTAX.

"Love, in itself, is very good,
But, 'tis by no means, solid food;
And ere our honey-moon was o'er,
I found we wanted something more.
This was the cause of all my trouble;
My income would not carry double;
But, led away from Reason's plan
By Love, that torturer of man,
In our delirium we forgot
What is Life's unremitted lot;
That man and woman, too, are born
Beneath each rose to find a thorn:
We thought, as other fools have done,
That Hymen's laws had made us one;
But had forgot that Nature, true
To her own purpose, made us two.
There were two mouths that daily cried,
At morn and eve, to be supplied:
Though by one vow we were betrothed,
There were two bodies to be clothed:
And, to improve my happiness,
Dolly is very fond of dress.
My head's content with one hat on it,
While Dorothy has hat and bonnet:
In short, there's no day passes through
But I, and my dear Doll, are two.
One good has my kind fortune sped:
Dolly, my Lord, has never bred.
Thus, though we're always Two, you see,
We haply yet have ne'er been THREE.

She came a beauty to my arms;
Her only dower was her charms:
But much she saved me, I must own,
By never bringing brats to town."

MY LORD.

"Another time, my reverend guest,
I hope you will relate the rest:
I truly wish the whole to know,
But business calls, and I must go.
I need not, sure, repeat my words:
Command whate'er the house affords."

The Peer thus with the Doctor parted,
And left him gay and easy-hearted;
While many a pipe his thoughts digest,
Till his eyes told the hour of rest.

When the next morn, and breakfast came,
Said Syntax, "I should be to blame,
If I delayed to tell my mind
To one so generous and so kind,
In hopes such counsel to receive
As he will condescend to give.
For as I on my bed reclined,
A sudden thought possessed my mind,
Which may produce, as I've a notion,
A North-West passage to promotion.

"Loyal and true I've ever been,
And much of this same world I've seen:
Well versed in the historic page
Of this and every other age,

I could employ my studious hour
For those who held the reins of power;
And sure a well-turned pamphlet might
Attention from the court invite;
By which I could, in nervous prose,
Unveil the ministerial foes;
And, with no common skill and care,
Praise and support the powers that are.
I then might be preferred at once,
No more the prey of any dunce,
Who views poor authors as mere drudges,
And every doit he pays them grudges;
Nor cares how much he makes them feel,
Just as a cook-maid skins an eel.
It would be better far I trow,
Than this same Paternoster-Row;
Where the poor bees in Learning's hive,
Toil, but to make the tradesmen thrive—
And for their intellectual honey,
Get but a poor return in money.
It would be cutting matters short,
Could I but get a friend at court:
'Twould be, and I repeat the notion,
A North-West passage to promotion."

MY LORD.

"Patient, my learned Doctor, hear;
And to my counsels give an ear:
I long have known, and known too well,
The country where you wish to dwell.
Corruption, fraud, and envy wait
At the proud Statesman's crowded gate;

There fawning flattery wins its way,
There the base passions join the fray,
Like beasts that on each other prey;
While the smile hides each traitorous
heart,
And interest plays a Proteus* part.
You've too much virtue, my good friend,
Your talents and your time to lend
To such a power—for such an end.
Can you work up the specious lie
That does not quite the Truth deny?
Can you that kind of Truth relate,
On which you may prevaricate?
Will you from others bear to seek
What you must think, and write, and
speak?
Will you, to-day, their systems borrow,
And calmly shake them off to-morrow?
Will you, cameleon-like, receive
The hue a Patron wants to give?
—You've too much honest pride to be
A scribbler to the Treasury,
Where you must wait the lagging hour,
And cringe to images of power;
To men in office, upstart elves,
Who think of little but themselves.

* L'Ingannare, il mentir, la fraude, il furto,
Et la rapinadi di pieta vestita;
Crescer col danno, e precipizio altrui,
E far a se de l'altrui biasmo more,
Son la virtu di quella gente infida.
PASTOR FIDO.

"When long an hackneyed slave you've
been,
And dashed and dived through thick and
thin;
When you have changed each purer thought
For morals which in courts are taught:
When all distinctions that belong
To what is right and what is wrong,
Have, of your reason, lost their hold,
For dribblets of a patron's gold;
When the bold Logic, framed by Truth,
Your filial boast in early youth,
Yields to the vacillating rule
Of policy's complying school;—
When guile and cunning, from your breast
Have driven that once-honoured guest,
You may, perhaps, or you may not
Be set aside, unheard, forget:
Or haply find, when Virtue's lost,
Repentance, and some petty post.
This will not do, my learned friend,
You must to better things attend;
All thoughts of Downing Street forego,
And stick to Paternoster Row.

"The man of trade you cannot blame,
For money is his native aim;
It is the object of all trade
To make as much as can be made:
Bankers and Booksellers alike,
At every point of profit strike;

And the same spirit you will meet
In Mincing Lane or Lombard Street.
'Tis not confined, we all must know,
To vulgar tradesmen in the Row.
Success depends on writing well—
Booksellers bow when volumes sell.
On the Exchange each day at three,
This self-same principle you'll see;
Lead thither the vast, pressing throng;
And know, dear Sir, or right or wrong,
'Tis that which makes Old England strong:
Though roguery in Vellum's shop,
It is, my friend, the Nation's prop:
And though you please, good Sir, to flout it,
Old England could not do without it.
Without it she might be as good,
But half as great she never would.
I look with pleasure to the fame
That now awaits your learned name,
And when your labours are well paid,
You'll be the Eulogist of Trade.

"Vellum may be a purse-proud Cit,
With more of money than of wit,
But Vellum, my good Sir, can tell
The kind of book that's made to sell.
Indeed, the man whose pocket's full,
However empty be his skull,
Although immeasurably dull,
Will find, 'midst the ill-judging crowd,
Far greater reason to be proud,

Than he whose head contains a store
Of critic skill, and learned lore,
If to his wit he does not join
The blest command of ready coin.
Write and get rich, nor fear the taunts
Of Booksellers and such gallants;
Vellum has no more sordid tricks
Than those who deal in Politics;
But till your various Learning's known,
And your works sell throughout the town;
Till, having settled Fortune's spite,
Your name shall sanction what you write,
Let Vellum his rewards bestow,
Nor scoff at PATERNOSTER ROW."

SYNTAX.

"To your kind words I've nought to say,
But thank your Lordship, and obey.
And now, as twenty years have passed
Since I beheld fair London last,
I shall employ the present day
In strolling calmly to survey
What changes Time and Chance have
made,
What Wealth has done, and Art essayed,
What Taste has, in its fancies, shown,
To give new splendour to the Town:
That being done, I'll take my way
To Covent Garden—to the play."

"Then," said his Lordship, "when we
meet,
I shall expect a special treat,

To hear my learned friend impart
His notions of dramatic art."

The Doctor bowed, and off he went,
Upon his curious progress bent:
He paced the Parks—he viewed each
Square,
And, staring, he made others stare.
At length, at the appointed hour,
He hastened to the Playhouse door,
And took his place within the pit,
Beside a critic and a wit,
As wits and critics now are known,
Who hash up nonsense for the Town;
And, in the daily columns, show
How small the sum of all they know.

"I think," said Syntax, looking round,
"It is not good, this vast profound:
I see no well-wrought columns here!
No attic ornaments appear;
Nought but a washy, wanton waste
Of gaudy tints and puny taste:
Too large to hear—too long to see—
Full of unmeaning symmetry.
The parts all answer one another;
Each pigeon-hole reflects its brother;
And all, alas! too plainly show
How easy 'tis to form a Row:
But where's the grand, the striking
whole?
A Theatre should have a soul."

"Excuse me, Sir," the critic said,
"These Theatres are all a trade:
Their owners laugh at scrolls and friezes;
'Tis a full house, alone, that pleases:
And you must know, it is the plan
To stick and stuff it as they can:
Your noble architectural graces
Would take up room, and fill up places."

"This may be true, Sir, to the letter;
But genius would have managed better,"
Syntax replied:—"Nay, I am willing
To let them gain the utmost shilling;
But surely talent might be found,
(The natives, too, of British ground,)
Who could have blended attic merit
With this proprietory spirit."

Thus as he spoke, the curtain rose,
And forced his harangue to a close:
But still, as they the drama viewed,
The conversation was renewed,
And lasted till the whole was o'er;
When, as they passed the Playhouse door,
The Critic said—"'Twill wound my heart
If you and I so soon must part:
O, how I long to crack a bottle
With such a friend of Aristotle!
Now, as you seem to know him well,
Perhaps his residence you'll tell."
"Where it is now I do not know,"
Syntax replied;—"and I must go;

But this I can most boldly say—
You'll never meet him at the play."

When fairly got into the street,
"O," thought the Doctor, "what a treat
For my good Lord, when next we meet!"

CANTO XXIV.

Now Syntax, as he travelled back,
Lolling and stretching in a hack,
Could not but wonder in his mind
On what he had just left behind.
"I've seen a play," he muttering said;
"'Twas Shakespeare's—but in masquerade.
I've seen a farce, I scarce know what;
'Twas only fit to be forgot.
I've seen a Critic, and have heard
The string of nonsense he preferred.
Heaven bless me! where has Learning fled?
Where has she hid her sacred head?
O how degraded is she grown,
To spawn such boobies on the town!
The sterling gold is seen no more;
In vain we seek the genuine ore:
Some mixture doth its worth debase;
Some wire-drawn nonsense takes its place.
How few consume the midnight oil!
How few in Learning's labour toil!
Content, as they incurious stray
Through Life's unprofitable day,
With straws that on the surface flow,
Nor look for pearls that live below:
They ne'er the hidden depths explore,
But gather sea-weed on the shore!

There was a period when the stage
Was thought to dignify the age;
When learned men were seen to sit
Upon the benches of the pit;
When, to his Art and Nature true,
GARRICK his various pictures drew;
While every passion, every thought,
He to perfection fully wrought,
By Nature's self supremely taught;
He did her very semblance bear,
And looked as she herself were there.
Whether old Lear's form he wore,
With age and sorrow covered o'er;
Or Romeo's amorous flame possessed,
That torture of the human breast;
Or gay Lothario's glowing pride,
In conquest o'er his rival's bride;
Or when, with fell ambition warm,
In Macbeth or in Gloster's form,
He gave each passion to the eye
In all its fine variety:
The words he did not loudly quote;
But acted e'en as SHAKESPEARE wrote.

"Nor was he less (for he could range
In every wayward busy change
Known in the field of scenic art—
The true cameleon of the heart)
When he assumed the merry glee
Of laughter-loving COMEDY.

"In Ranger's tricks, or when he strove
In Benedict to hide his love;

When he in Drugger's doublet shone,
Or Brute's rude ribaldry put on;
When he the jealous Kitely played;
When the same passion he essayed
In Felix;—with what truth and force
He urged that passion's different course,
Worked up its features all anew—
But still he was to Nature true!
Nay, e'en in Farce he could awake
The fun that made the galleries shake,
The heart he cheated of its woe,
And made the poignant tear to flow;
Lit up a joy in every eye,
Or drowned the soul in agony.
He ever was to Nature true;—
By no false arts did he subdue
The attentive mind, the listening ear;
In all the Drama's wild career,
He ne'er outstepped the unerring rule,
Which he had learned in Nature's school:
In every part he did excel;
He aimed at all, and all was well.
In those good times none went to see
The mere effects of scenery:
The constant laugh, the forced grimace,
The vile distortions of the face.
In those good times none went to see
Pierots and Clowns in Comedy.
Men sought perfection to discern,
And learned Critics went to learn.

"SHAKESPEARE, immortal Bard sublime!
Unmatched within the realm of time!
He did not with Promethean aim,
Attempt to steal æthereal flame;
Rather to him the thoughts of Heaven
Were, by Celestial bounty, given.
He read profound, in every page
Of Nature's volume, every age
And act of man! Each passion's course
He traces with resistless force;
Nay, with a more than mortal art,
Gives unknown feelings to the heart;
And doth the willing Fancy bear,
Just as his magic wills—and where.

"His page still lives, and sure will last
Till Time and all its years are past.
The Poet, to the end of Time,
Breathes in his works, and lives in rhyme;
But, when the Actor sinks to rest
And the turf lies upon his breast,
A poor traditionary fame
Is all that's left to grace his name.
The Drama's children strut and play,
In borrowed parts their lives away;
And then they share the obvious lot;
Smith will, like Cibber, be forgot!
Cibber, with fascinating art,
Could wake the pulses of the heart;
But hers is an expiring name,
And darling Smith's will be the same.

Of GARRICK's self e'en nought remains;
His art and him one grave contains:
In others' minds to make him live,
Is all remembrance now can give;
All we can say—alas! how vain!
We ne'er shall see his like again."

Just as this critic-speech was o'er,
The coach stopped at his Lordship's door:
But my good Lord was gone to bed;
So Syntax to his chamber sped—
Where, with his pipe, and o'er his bottle,
He chewed the cud of Aristotle,
Till, stretched upon his bed of down,
Sleep did his head with poppies crown;
And well he slept until a voice
Desired to know if 'twas his choice
Still to sleep on? And then it stated—
His Lordship and the breakfast waited.

"Well," said my Lord when he appeared,
"I hope the play your spirits cheered;
Falstaff, the morning critics tell,
Was never surely played so well."
"These critics," Syntax smiling said,
"Are wretched bunglers at their trade;
One sat beside me in the Pit,
No more a critic than a wit.
Between the acts we both expressed
Or what was worst, or what was best;
And whirled those intervals away
In changing thoughts upon the play;

And, though both formed to disagree,
Nought passed but perfect courtesy.
Perhaps it may your fancy suit
To hear our classical dispute:
I think, my Lord, 'twould prove a treat,
Should you allow me to repeat
All that this criticising sage
Knew of the humours of the stage:
For, as to what should form a play;
How actors should their parts convey;
What are the Drama's genuine laws,
The source from whence true Genius draws
Such scenes as when to Nature shown,
She loud exclaims—They are my own;
He knew no more, it will appear,
Than the tea-urn that's boiling here;
Like that, he did no more than bubble,
And without any toil or trouble:
They felt the trouble who sat near him;
And, sure enough, 'twas toil to hear him.
After some general trifling chat
Of the new Playhouse, and all that,
The scenes that passed before our eyes
Produced these questions and replies:
In short, I'll state our *quids* pro *quos*
Just in the order as they rose."

CRITIC.

"Oh, what a Falstaff!—Oh, how fine!
Oh, 'tis great acting—'tis divine."

SYNTAX.

"The acting's great—that I can tell ye;
For all his acting's in his belly."

CRITIC.

"But, with due deference to your joke,
A truer word I never spoke
Than when I say—you've never been
The witness of a finer scene.
The admired actor whom you see
Plays the fat Knight most charmingly:
'Tis in this part he doth excel;
Quin never played it half so well."

SYNTAX.

"You ne'er saw Quin the stage adorn:
He acted ere your sire was born;
The critics, Sir, who lived before you,
Would have disclosed a different story.
This play I've better acted seen
In country towns where I have been:
I do not hesitate to say—
I'd rather read this very play
By my own parlour fire-side,
With my poor judgment for my guide,
Than see the actors of this stage,
Who make me gape at Shakespeare's
page.
When I read Falstaff to myself,
I laugh like any merry elf:
While my mind feels a cheering glow
That Shakespeare only can bestow.

The swaggering words in his defence,
Which scarce are wit, and yet are sense;
The ribald jest—the quick conceit—
The boast of many a braggart feat:
The half-grave questions and replies,
In his high-wrought soliloquies;
The obscene thought—the pleasant prate,
Which give no time to love or hate.
In such succession do they flow,
From no to yea—from yea to no,
Have not been to my mind conveyed
By this pretender to his trade.
The smile sarcastic, and the leer
That tells the laughing mockery near;
The warning look, that, ere 'tis spoke,
Aptly forebodes the coming joke;
The air so solemn, yet so sly,
Shaped to conceal the ready lie;
The eyes, with some shrewd meaning
bright,
I surely have not seen to-night.
Again I must beg leave to tell ye,
'Tis nought of Falstaff but his belly."

CRITIC.

"All this is fine—and may be true;
But with such truths I've nought to do.
I'm sure, Sir, I shall say aright,
When I declare the great delight
The enraptured audience feel to-night.
It is indeed, with no small sorrow,
I cannot your opinions borrow
To fill the columns of to-morrow.

My light critique will be preferred,
The public always take my word:
Nay the loud plaudits heard around
Must all your far-fetched thoughts confound:
I truly wonder when I see,
You do not laugh as well as me."

SYNTAX.

"My muscles other ways are drawn;
I cannot laugh, Sir,—while I yawn."

CRITIC.

"But you will own the scenes are fine."

SYNTAX.

"Whate'er the acting, they're divine,
And fit for any pantomime.
Of this it is that I complain;
These are the tricks which I disdain:
The painter's art the play commends;
On gaudy show success depends.
The clothes are made in just design;
They're all well charactered and fine.
The actors now, I think, Heaven bless 'em,
Must learn their art from those who dress 'em;
But give me actors, give me plays,
On which I could with rapture gaze,
Though coats and scenes were made of baize:
For, if the scene were highly wrought;
If players acted as they ought;
You would not then be pleased to see
This heavy mass of frippery.
Hear Horace, Sir, who wrote of plays
In Ancient Rome's Augustan days:—

'Tanto cum strepitu ludi spectantur, et artes,
Divitiæque peregrinæ: quibus oblitus actor
Cum stetit in Scena, concurrit dextera lævæ.
Dixit adhuc aliquid? nil sane. Quid placet
ergo?
Lana Tarentino violas imitata veneno.' "

CRITIC.

"Your pardon, Sir, but all around me,
There are such noises they confound me;
And, though I full attention paid,
I scarcely know a word you said.
To say the truth, I must acknowledge
'Tis long since I have left the college:
Virgil and Horace are my friends,
I have them at my fingers' ends;
But Grecian lore, I blush to own,
Is wholly to my mind unknown.
I therefore must your meaning seek:
Oblige me, Sir, translate your Greek.
But see the farce is now begun,
And you must listen to the fun.
It sure has robbed you of your bile;
For now methinks, you deign to smile."

SYNTAX.

"The thing is droll, and aptly bent
To raise a vulgar merriment:
But Merry-Andrews, seen as such,
Have often made me laugh as much.
An Actor does but play the fool
When he forsakes old Shakespeare's rule,

And lets his own foul nonsense out,
To please the ill-judging rabble rout:
But when he swears, to furnish laughter,
The beadle's whip should follow after.
There's Terence, Sir, and then there's
Plautus;
They've both a better lesson taught us."

CRITIC.

"Terence, I know, he wrote in Latin,
Just as a weaver makes his satin.
He well deserved the comic bays:
For Westminster he wrote his plays:
And Plautus was a fellow famous,
He wrote a play called Ignoramus;
Where Lawyers by profession bold,
In Latin and in English scold."

"At length, my Lord, the parley ended:
Which, to amuse, cannot be mended.
You well may laugh so loud, but I
Feel myself more disposed to cry
When thus I see what asses sit
In judgment upon works of wit.

"I own, my Lord, I love a play—
When some performer's turned away,
By Green-Room tyrants, from the boards
Of London stage, our town affords
To tempt or him or her to stay
For a few nights, upon their way:
Then Doll and I are seen to sit
Conspicuous in our Country Pit."

Thus as he spoke, with frequent bows,
And fifty whens, and wheres, and hows,
Vellum appeared, with solemn look,
To talk about the Doctor's Book.
He said, "'Twas true a learned friend
The Manuscript did much commend:
He thinks it is a work of merit,
Written with learning, taste, and spirit;
The sketches too, if he don't err,
Possess appropriate character;
'Tis to the humour of our age,
And has your Lordship's patronage;
I therefore wish the work to buy,
And deal with liberality.
'Tis true that paper's very dear,
And workmen's wages most severe.
The volume's heavy, and demands
The engraver's and the printer's hands:
Besides, there is a risk to run:
Before the press its work has done,
New taxes may, perhaps, be laid
On some prime article of trade,
And then the price will be so high;—
The persons are but few who buy
Books of so very costly kind:
But still the work is to my mind.
I'll try my luck, and will be bound
To give, my Lord, three hundred pound."

After some little tricks of trade,
The bargain was completely made—
The work transferred, the money paid.

"Though," said my Lord, "I think
your gains
By no means equal to your pains;
(For Vellum will a bargain drive
As well as any man alive;)
The work will give my friend a name,
And stamp his literary fame;
'Twill Paternoster-Row command,
And keep old Vellum cap-in-hand:
And when a name is up, 'tis said,
The owner may lie snug in bed.
Write on—the learned track pursue—
And Booksellers shall cringe to you."

Much passed upon his Lordship's part,
Which showed the goodness of his heart;
While Syntax made his full replies,
Not with his tongue—but with his eyes.

CANTO XXV.

My Lord retired—the Doctor too,
As he had nothing else to do,
Thought he would take a peep and see
His noble Patron's Library.
So down he sat, without a care,
In a well-stuffed Morocco chair,
And seized a book; but Morpheus shed
The poppies o'er his reverend head;
While fancy would not be behind;
So played her tricks within his mind,
And furnished a most busy dream
Which Syntax made his pleasant theme,
Soon as he met my Lord to dine,
Or rather while they took their wine.

THE DREAM.

That I was in the Strand I dreamed,
And o'er my head methought there seemed
A flight of volumes in the air,
In various bindings gilt and fair:
The unfolded leaves, exposed to view,
Served them as wings on which they flew.
In the mid air they passed along
In stately flight a numerous throng,
And from each book a label fell,
Formed every author's name to tell.

Nor was it long before I saw,
With a fond, reverential awe,
The celebrated Bards and Sages
Which graced the Greek and Roman ages,
All headed by a solemn fowl
Which bore the semblance of an Owl.
'Twas Pallas' Bird, who led them straight
Through Temple-Bar's expanded Gate.
—Year-Books, Reports, and sage grave
Entries,
At either Temple-gate stood sentries:
While Viner his Abridgement shows
In sixty well-armed Folios.
The Lamb, it baaed, the Horse, it neighed,
In reverence of the cavalcade.
Near Clifford's-Inn appeared to stand
Of Capiases an ugly band;
For when their parchment flags appeared,
Instant the crowded street was cleared;
And the procession passed along,
Untroubled by a pressing throng.
St. Dunstan's savages were mute,
But still they gave their best salute;
Disdaining Eloquence and Rhymes,
They 'woke their bells to speak in chimes.
Erskine's famed Pamphlet Cap-a-pee,
With many an I, and many a Me,
Issued from Serjeants'-Inn, and made
A speech to grace the grand parade.
The Stationers came forth to meet
The stranger forms in Ludgate-street,

Each one, upon his brawny back,
Bearing a large sheet Almanack.
For a short time the Learned train
Stopped before Ave-Maria-Lane,
That Galen might just view the College,
The seat of medicinal knowledge.
Nor did they fail awhile to tarry
Before St. Paul's learned Seminary,
Where Lilly's Grammar did rehearse
Propria quæ Maribus in verse.
At Cheapside-end there seemed to stand
A pageant rather huge than grand,
Ream upon Ream of Quire stock
Appeared like some vast, massive rock:
On its firm base a figure stood,
A composite of brass and wood:
The months and weeks around it stand,
With each a number in its hand
Of Bibles, Histories, and Reviews,
And Magazines from every Muse,
With coverlids of various hue,
Pea-green and red, and brown and blue.
The shape was clad in Livery-gown;
The face had neither smile nor frown,
While it held out a monstrous paunch
As fat with many a ham and haunch,
Two Printer's Devils o'er his head
A crimson canvas widely spread,
Whereon was writ in gilded show—
" GENIUS OF PATERNOSTER-ROW."
The mighty Giants of Guildhall,
Urged by a sympathetic call,

No sooner heard the clock strike One,
Than from their stations they came down,
And in Cheapside they took their stand,
In honour of the Classic Band,
But when they heard the clock strike Two,
Marched back as they were wont to do.
Now as they came near the Old-Jewry,—
Like Dulness worked into a Fury,
A vulgar shape appeared, who flew
On pinions marked with ONE and TWO,
And other items which denote
That four pence is well worth a groat.
It seemed to lead a numerous train
Who rendered further passage vain.
Straight he came forward to produce
A Blank-Sheet as a flag of truce.
Near him two fluttering Pamphlets bore
Standards, with figures covered o'er:
A gilt Pence-table graced the one,
The Price of Stocks on t'other shone.
A picquet guard of Valuations,
And Interest Tables took their stations
Around their leader, who drew nigh,
To make his bold soliloquy;
But, ere he speaks, my proper course is
Just to describe the City Forces.

Bill-Books and Cash-Books formed the
van,
An active and a numerous clan:
The Journals followed them, whose skill
Is exercised in daily drill:

On either side appeared to range
Unpaid Accounts, Bills of Exchange,
And files of Banker's Checks: these three
Manœuvred as Light Infantry;
While every other trading book
Its regular position took:
And Quires of Blotting Paper stood
To suck up any flow of blood.
The Ledgers the main body form,
Armed to resist the coming storm;
Whose ponderous shapes could boldly
show
A steady phalanx to the foe.

Discord appeared with base intent
The hostile spirit to foment:
Not Discord that precedes the car
Of Mars whene'er he goes to war,
But of a different rank and nation,
Known by the name of Litigation;
Born on some foul Attorney's desk;
Bred but to harass and perplex;
Whose appetite is for dispute,
And has no wish but for a suit.
She rose upon a Gander's wing,
And round about began to fling
Pleas, Declarations, and each bit
Of Parchment that could form a Writ.

The Newspapers, with pen in hand,
In the balconies took their stand;
Waiting with that impartial spirit,
Which all well know they all inherit,

To make the hurry of the Battle
Through all the next day's columns rattle;
And, with one conscience, to prepare
The History of this Paper war.

The Herald now the silence broke,
'Twas mighty COCKER's self that spoke;
And thus to Pallas' Bird addressed
The solemn purpose of his breast.

"I state my claim to ask and know
From whence you come and where you go,
And by what license you appear
With all your foreign Pagans here?
Come you with all this Cavalcade
To insult the Vehicles of Trade;
And our dear home-bred rights invade?
A mighty force awaits you here,
To check and punish your career;
And I am ordered by my masters,
Who fear disturbance and disasters,
To bid you quickly turn about,
From London streets to take your route,
Or we shall quickly turn you out.
My name is COCKER, which is known
In every Counting-house in Town:
Nay, such my use and reputation,
I am respected through the nation.
Yes, I'm the Father, I who speak,
Of Mercantile Arithmetic;
Source of a race that far outvies
Your Greek and Latin progenies:

And now I hope that in a crack
You'll send an humble answer back,
Or else expect a fierce attack.
I'll count twice two, and then add four,
That time I'll give, but give no more.
One, two, three, four, five, six, seven,
eight,—
I've done, and will no longer wait."

The Bird of Pallas, who could speak
In English or in Attic Greek
As suited best—did not prolong
His answer in the Vulgar Tongue.

"'Twas a Petition, duly made
By certain of your Sons of Trade,
To beg my mistress would permit
That they should buy a little Wit;
And here import, though in defiance
Of common rules, a little Science.
I ask not, if 'twas their intent
To gain a name—or ten per cent.;
Whether 'tis wisdom or misdoing;
Whether 'twill prove their good or ruin,
Or the result of civic sense,
Or a shrewd, mercantile pretence:
Whether 'tis Interest or Pride
That turns them from old rules aside:
That urges them to tax their trade,
For offerings to the Immortal Maid;
These self-same matters, to be free,
Are, Mister Cocker, nought to me.

'Tis by Minerva's high command,
That I conduct this Classic Band;
'Tis she commands, and we obey;
Nor shall you stop us on the way,
Whether it does or does not suit
Your pleasure, to the INSTITUTE
We'll go, you calculating brute.
Say, will your low-born volumes dare
With these brave veterans to compare?
What's all this bustle—all this fuss?
Think you they can contend with us?
They who are slaves, so base and willing,
Of any pound, and pence, and shilling:
As the pen gives they're forced to drink
The venal dips of any ink;
And when they're filled, their lives expire,
Consigned to light a kitchen fire;
Or sent away to such vile use
As Chandlers or as Hucksters choose.
If they oppose our stated way,
We'll sweep them from the face of day.

"At the same time we wish for peace,
And that your saucy threats may cease.
We do not mean to mock the City
With any hope of being witty;
We do not bring our learned powers
To vex its speculating hours;
Or with poetic visions cross
Your schemes of Profit and of Loss.
We did not first suggest the deed,
To bring you books you cannot read.

Meetings were formed and speeches made,
And all by weighty men of trade,
To frame the unforeseen request;
And surely we have done our best,
When we each Classic did provide,
With a Translation by its side.
Dryden is ready to rehearse
All Virgil's works in English verse;
And Grecian Homer rests his hope
Of being understood by Pope.
Leland will give you, if ye please,
The speeches of Demosthenes;
While Northern Güthrie will bestow
The eloquence of Cicero.
To Thomas Styles and John a Nokes,
Carr will repeat old Lucian's Jokes.
While Juvenal's sharp satire shines
In William Giffard's rival lines.
Coleman and Thornton will convey
Right notions of a Latin Play.
Whate'er the ancient Critics wrote,
You now may in plain English quote!
And drink Pye's health, when o'er the
bottle,
For Anglicising Aristotle:
Nay, all the Ancient Bards have sung
You now may sing in Vulgar Tongue.
What could we more?—so cease your riot,
And let us pass along in quiet.
Dismiss your Counting-house parade;
Send off these cumbrous tomes of trade:

Back to their counters let them roam,
And sip their ink, and stay at home;
Nor e'er again their threats oppose
To Grecian and to Roman foes."

COCKER.

"Fools may be found, I do not doubt it,
Within this City as without it:
This truth, indeed, is very clear,
For they were fools who brought you here.
I pray thee tell me what has wit
To do with any plodding cit!
Of wit we know not what is meant,
Unless 'tis found in Cent. per Cent.
Learning, a drug has always been;
No Warehouseman will take it in.
Should practised Mercers quit their satin
To look at Greek and long for Latin?
Should the pert, upstart Merchant's boy
Behold the Tower, and think of Troy?
Or should a Democratic Hatter
'Bout old Republics make a clatter?
Should City Praters leave their tools,
To talk by Ciceronian rules;
And at our meetings in Guildhall
Puzzle the mob with Classic brawl?
No, to such things they've no pretence;
No—let them stick to common sense:—
You may your Ancient Bards rehearse,
But there's no common sense in verse;
Not all the Classics at your tail
Would weigh an ounce in Reason's scale.

I treat the name of Rome with scorn;
Give me the Commerce of Leghorn.
From Italy's prolific shore,
The wondrous science was brought o'er,
The bright invention which conveyed
Such vast facilities of Trade;
The Double Entry far outvies
All pictured, sculptured fantasies:
And sure I am, his honoured name
Deserves a brighter wreath of Fame,
To whose kind mind the scheme occurred,
Than e'er was won by conqueror's sword.
What did the Greeks, pray, know of trade?
Ulysses, as I've heard it said,
Was full ten months obliged to roam,
Before he brought his cargo home:
A voyage in that self-same sea,
Our coasting brigs would make in three.
The Institution was displayed
As a mere trumpery trick of trade,
Decked out, 'tis true, with great parade;
While you are coming as a bribe,
To make our purse-proud cits subscribe;
And aid the primary intent
Of dividends of ten per cent.
We have our pedant tradesmen too,
Who talk as if they something knew,
And Learning's cud pretend to chew:
Who get cramp words, and court the Muse
In Magazines and in Reviews.
Yes, we have those whose priggish rage is,
Not to read books—but title-pages:

We spare no cost in drink and meat
To furnish out a tempting treat
That may attract an attic train
To Mincing or to Philpot Lane;
Who snatch the feast, and go away
To mock the patron of the day.
There are who strive to have it thought,
That they have minds with Learning fraught:
Though, if they have so small discerning,
To interrupt their trade with Learning;
The day will come when they'll be found
With certain shillings in the pound.
But to be brief—consult your fame,
And go back gravely, as you came:
Or we shall send you somewhat faster,
Nor for your wounds afford a plaster.
—Look at that form which soars in air,
And shines like a portentous star;
It is the armorial symbol bright,
Of a renowned, commercial Knight,
Who sought not a superior fame
Than doth befit a Merchant's name.
See how his ensign is unfurled
O'er the Emporium of the world,
And does with threatening aspect view
Your Owlish worship and your Crew;
While in its motions we descry
The sure presage of Victory.
Yes, on success I calculate,
As sure as four and four make eight.

Thus I have clearly stated the amount,
Errors excepted, of my just account."

THE OWL.

"Good Mister Cocker, I have heard
All that your wisdom has preferred;
And I entreat you turn your head,
In which such numbers have been bred,
And see an Eastern wind prevail,
To make your grasshopper turn tail;
From which my wise soothsayer draws
An omen fatal to your cause;
And you may hear his tongue proclaim,
'Your boobies will all do the same.'
But talking is of little use—
Therefore at once I break the truce."

As Critics now when called to duel,
Disdainful of the common fuel,
No more with shot or bullet vapour,
But wound with ink, and kill with paper.
Both sides for conflict dire prepare;
And thus commenced the threatened war.

Euclid at Master Cocker flew,
Whom by one stroke he overthrew;
Then with a knotty problem bound him,
And left him struggling where he found
him.
Cæsar, with all his Latins, pounced
On the light parties, whom they trounced,
And soon a dreadful havoc made
Of bills that never would be paid:

While Banker's Cheques made quick retreat,
And huddled into Lombard Street.
With equal force the Greeks attack,
And drove the heavy legions back;
Ledgers and Journals lay all scattered:
Bill-Books and Cash-Books were bespattered.
Short was the contest; struck with dread,
Confused the City forces fled.
For aid on Stationers they call,
But they were busy at their Hall;
And this same Hall their trade-craft found
To be a sort of neutral ground:
For they conceived the havoc made,
Might serve the paper-making trade:
To side with either they were loth,
In hopes to profit from them both.

The Postman now his clarion blew;
His blasts were vain—they would not do;
The Letter-Books disordered flew:
While Pindar from Bow-steeple clock
Looked down, and, as he viewed the shock,
Chanted, nor did he chant in vain,
A loud and animating strain.
Forth from the Bank a troop was sent
Of threes and fours and fives per cent.,
But they ran off, nor struck a blow;
For Stocks that day were very low.
The Policies remained secure,
Waiting for arms of signature;

For what brave spirit e'er would fight 'em
When nobody would underwrite 'em.

And now these doughty cits were beat,
Down every lane, up every street;
But met to form each broken rank,
Before the Portals of the Bank:
There they a solemn council hold,
Whether by added strength grown bold,
To a new contest they should come,
Or sneak away disbanded home.

Thus the old Classics having beat
The vulgar foe, sought Coleman Street:
But as they passed, a numerous host
At Coopers' Hall, had taken post.
Two blue-coat urchins played the fife
Which called them to the martial strife;
When, 'stead of pointed darts and lances,
They pelted the Antiques with Chances.
But Fortune, who is ever blind,
Turned short and left her bands behind:
Their Leader lost, away they steal,
And hide their numbers in the Wheel.

At length the Classic Sages greet
Their Parthenonian retreat:
But while the echoing walls around
With Io Pæans loud resound;
Again the vengeful foes appeared,
Again their angry standards reared.
"Must we once more," the Ancients said,
"O'ercome these frantic imps of. trade?

Is there no power to save our race
From war, when conquest is disgrace?"
The Greeks then called on PORSON'S name:
The Latins echoed back the same;
And straight in Grecian stole arrayed,
Appeared the venerable shade.
Homer went down upon his knees,
And so did tragic Sophocles,
With all the names that end in ῆs.

"Hail, sacred tomes!" he said, "to you
I grateful owed whate'er I knew:
From you I gained my mortal fame;
The honours of a scholar's name:
To you the immortal power I owe,
To give the aid I now bestow:
I come from that Celestial Hall
Where they all dwell who wrote you all."
He spoke—and lo! a volume came,
Of size immense and rueful name:
Its back no verbal title bore;
But numerous dates of time long o'er;
While on its lettered sides appears,
"LONDON GAZETTES for FIFTY YEARS!!"
Straight to the foe, that, all aloof,
Fluttered about each neighbouring roof,
It did full many a page unfold,
And showed Whereas, and cried, "Behold!"
While that same word, upon the walls
Blazed forth in flaming Capitals.
Whereas a thousand voices rung,
And on the wing there upwards sprung

A flight of Dockets, who were joined
By dire Certificates unsigned:
These saw the foes, and, chilled with
  dread,
Trembled and shrieked aloud, and fled.

The Ghost now vanished from the
  view;
The Bird of Pallas vanished too.
And then I thought, the Classic elves
Instinctive sought their proper shelves,
Where undisturbed each learned Tome
May slumber till the Day of Doom.
I woke and felt a real glee
At this same fancied victory.
Nor would I change my Classic lore,
Poor as I am, for all the store,
Which plodding anxious trade can give,
In constant doubt and fear to live.
My treasures are all well secured,
I want them not to be insured:
My Greek and Latin are immured
Within the warehouse of my brain,
And there in safety they remain.
My little cargo's lodged at home,
Where storms and tempests never come.

Learning will give an unmixed pleasure,
Which gold can't buy, and trade can't
  measure;
But each within his destined station:
Learning's my pride and consolation,

That high-formed inmate of the soul,
Which, as the changing seasons roll,
Acquires new strength, preserves its
power,
And smiles in life's extremest hour.
The learned man, let who will flout him;
Doth always carry it about him;
And should he idly fail to use it,
Though it may rust, he will not lose it:
Fortune may leave off her caressing,
But she can't rob him of that blessing
Full many a comfort money gives;
But ask him who for money lives,
Whether he other pleasures shares,
Than sordid joys and golden cares?

How oft I've passed an evening hour
Within an hawthorn's humble bower,
And read aloud each charming line,
That doth in Virgil's Georgics shine:
Though Wealth passed by in stately
guise,
I felt no rankling envy rise;
Nor could the show my mind engage
From the Immortal Poet's page.
When homeward as I used to stray,
Along the unfrequented way;
Enraptured, as I strolled along,
With Philomela's evening song,
I felt what worldlings never share;
Oblivion of all human care:

Such hours are few, but well we know,
That Learning can those hours bestow.

My Lord continued the debate;
And time passed on in pleasant prate,
Till night broke up the tete-a-tete.

CANTO XXVI.

CROWNED with success, the following day
The Doctor homeward took his way;
And on the morrow, he again
Was borne by Grizzle o'er the plain.
But Grizzle, having lived in clover,
Symptoms of spirit did discover,
That more than once had nearly thrown
Her deep-reflecting master down,
Nor, till they'd travelled half the day,
Did he perceive he'd lost his way:
Nor to that moment, did he find,
That Grizzle, by some chance unkind,
Had left her ears and tail behind.
"Ne'er mind, good beast," he kindly said:
"What though no ears bedeck your head;
What though the honours of your rump
Are dwindled to a naked stump;
Now raised in purse as well as spirit,
Your master will reward your merit."
Another day they journeyed on;
The next, and lo! the work was done.

Some days before, (I had forgot
To say,) a letter had been wrote,
To tell how soon he should appear,
And re-embrace his dearest dear:

But not one solitary word
Of his good fortune he preferred.

"Yes, home is home, where'er it be,
Or shaded by the village-tree;
Or where the lofty domes arise,
To catch the passing stranger's eyes."
'Twas thus he thought, when at the gate
He saw his Doll impatient wait;
Nor, as he passed the street along,
Was he unnoticed by the throng;
For not a head within a shop
But did through door or window pop.
He kissed his Dame, and gravely spoke;
For now he brooded o'er a joke;
While she to know impatient burned
With how much money he returned.
"Give me my pipe," he said, "and ale,
And in due time you'll hear the tale."

He sat him down his pipe to smoke,
Looked sad, and not a word he spoke;
But Madam soon her speech began,
And in discordant tones it ran.

"I think, by that confounded look,
You have not writ your boasted book;
Yes, all your money you have spent,
And come back poorer than you went:
Yes, you have wandered far from home,
And here a beggar you are come;
But bills from all sides are in waiting,
To give your Reverence a baiting.

I do not mean to scold and rail;
But I'll not live with you in jail.
So long a time you've stayed away,
That the town curate you must pay;
For, while from home you played the fool,
He kindly came to teach the school;
And a few welcome pounds to earn
By flogging boys, to make them learn:
But I must say, you silly elf,
You merit to be flogged yourself;
And I've a mind this whip shall crack
Upon your raw-boned, lazy back.
Yes, puff away—but 'tis no joke
For all my schemes to end in smoke.
What, tongue-tied booby! will you say
To Mrs. Dress'em?—Who will pay
Her bills for these nice clothes?—Why
zounds!
It borders upon twenty pounds."

Thus, as she vehemently prated,
And the delighted Doctor rated,
From a small pocket in his coat,
He unobserved drew forth a note,
And, throwing it upon the table,
He said, "My dear, you'll now be able
To keep your mantua-maker quiet;
So cease, I beg, this idle riot:
And, if you'll not make such a pother,
I'll treat you with its very brother.
Be kind—and I'll not think it much
To show you half-a-dozen such."

She started up in joy's alarms,
And clasped the Doctor in her arms;
Then ran to bid the boys huzza,
And gave them all a holiday.

"Such is the matrimonial life,"
Said Syntax:—"but I love my wife.
Just now with horsewhip I was bothered;
And now with hugging I am smothered;
But wheresoe'er I'm doomed to roam,
I still shall say—that home is home!"

Again her dear the Dame caressed,
And clasped him fondly to her breast.
At length amidst her amorous play,
The Doctor found a time to say—
"The fatted calf I trust you've slain,
To welcome Syntax home again:"
"No," she replied, "no fatted calf;
We have a better thing by half;
For, with expectation big
Of your return, we killed a pig:
And a rich hazlet at the fire,
Will give you all you can desire:
The savory meat myself will baste,
And suit it to my deary's taste."
"That dish," he cried, "I'd rather see,
Than fricandeau or fricassee.
O," he continued, "what a blessing
To have a wife so fond of dressing;
Who with such taste and skill can work,
To dress herself and dress the pork!"

She now returned to household care,
The dainty supper to prepare.

Whoe'er has passed an idle hour,
In following Syntax through his Tour,
Must have perceived he did not balk
His fancy, when he wished to talk:
Nay, more—that he was often prone
To make long speeches when alone;
And while he quaffed the inspiring ale,
Between each glass to tell a tale:
Or, as he smoked with half-shut eyes,
Now smiling, and now looking wise,
He'd crack a joke or moralize:
And when this curious spirit stirred him,
He minded not though no one heard him.
This he did now—as 'twill appear;
He talked though there were none to hear;
When the whiffs passed, he silence broke,
And thus he thought, and puffed, and
spoke:

THE SMOKING SOLILOQUY.

"That man, I trow, is doubly curst,
Who of the best doth make the worst;
And he, I'm sure, is doubly blest,
Who of the worst can make the best.
To sit in sorrow and complain,
Is adding folly to our pain.

"In adverse state there is no vice
More mischievous than cowardice;

'Tis by resistance that we claim
The Christian's venerable name.
If you resist him, e'en Old Nick
Gives up his meditated trick:
Fortune contemns the whining slave,
And loves to smile upon the brave.

"In all this self-same chequered strife
We meet with in the road of life,
Whate'er the object we pursue,
There's always something to subdue;
Some foe, alas! to evil prone,
In others' bosoms or our own.
That man, alone, is truly great,
Who nobly meets the frowns of Fate,
Who, when the threatening tempests lower,
When the clouds burst in pelting shower,
When lightnings flash along the sky,
And thunders growl in sympathy,
With calmness to the scene conforms,
Nor fears nor mocks the angry storms:
He does not run, all helter-skelter,
To seek a temporary shelter;
Nor does he fume, and fret, and foam,
Because he's distant far from home;
For well he knows, each peril past,
He's sure to find a home at last.

"If petty evils round you swarm,
Let not their buzz your temper warm,
But brush them from your mind away,
Like insects of a summer's day.

"Evil oppose with Reason's power,
Nor fear the dark or threatening hour:
Combat the world;—but, as 'tis fit,
To the decrees of Heaven submit.

"If Spite and Malice are your foes,
If fell Revenge its arrow throws,
Look calmly on, nor fear the dart;
Virtue will guard the honest heart:
Nor let your angry spirit burn
The pointed missile to return.
The good man never fails to wield
A broad and strong protecting shield,
That will preserve him through the strife
Which never fails to trouble life;
And, when he meets his final doom,
Will form a trophy for his tomb.

"Bear and forbear—a dogma true
As human wisdom ever drew.
If you would lighten every care,
And every sorrow learn to bear,
To be secure from vile disgrace,
Look frowning Fortune in the face;
And, if the foe's too strong, retreat,
But not as if you had been beat:
Calmly avoid the o'erpowering fray,
Nor fight when you can stalk away;
For you can scarce be said to yield,
If, when you slowly quit the field,
You so present yourself to view,
That a wise foe will not pursue.

"I, who have long been doomed to
drudge,
Without a patron or a judge;
I, who have seen the booby rise
To dignified pluralities,
While I his flock to virtue steer,
For hard-earned thirty pounds a-year;
A flock, alas! he does not know,
But by the fleeces they bestow:
I who have borne the heaviest fate
That doth on Learning's toil await;
For when a man's the sport of Heaven
To keep a school the fellow's driven;
(Nor when that thought gay Lucian spoke,
He did not mean to crack a joke;*—)
I still man's dignity maintained,
And though I felt, I ne'er complained.

"If life's a farce, mere children's play,
Let the rich trifle it away:
I cannot model mine by theirs,
For mine has been a life of cares.

"Men with superior minds endowed
May soar above the titled crowd,
Though 'tis their humble lot to dwell
In calm retirement's distant cell:—

* Lucian says, that when the gods make a man the object of their sportive persecutions, they turn him into a schoolmaster. Such an one as Doctor Syntax was, may think, that the sarcastic Greek is in the right; but the Masters of Eton, Westminster, and Winchester, are, probably, of a different opinion.

Or by dame Fortune poorly fed,
To call on science for their bread;
To lead the life that I have led:—
Though neither wealth nor state is given,
They're the Nobility of Heaven.

"In its caprice a Sovereign's power
May make a noble every hour:
A King may only speak the word,
And some rich blockhead struts a Lord;
But all the sceptred powers that live
Cannot one ray of genius give.
Heaven and Nature must combine
To make the flame of genius shine;
Of wealth regardless or degree,
It may be sent to shine on me.
Learning, I thank thee;—though by toil
And the pale lamp of midnight oil
I gained thy smiles; though many a year
Fortune refused my heart to cheer;
By the inspiring laurels crowned,
I oft could smile while Fortune frowned.
Beguiled by thee, I oft forgot
My uncombed wig and rusty coat:
When coals were dear, and low my fire,
I warmed myself with Homer's lyre:
Or, in a dearth of ale benign,
I eager quaffed the stream divine,
Which flows in Virgil's every line.
To save me from domestic brawls
I thundered Tully to the walls:

When nought I did could Dolly please,
I laughed with Aristophanes,—
And oft has Grizzle, on our way,
Heard me from Horace smart and gay.

"Though with the world I struggled
hard,
Virtue my best, but sole reward;
When my whole income could but keep
The wolf from preying on the sheep;
Ne'er would I change my classic store
For all that Crœsus had, or more;
Nor would I lose what I have read,
Though tempting Fortune in its stead,
Would shower down mitres on my head.

"Bear and forbear,—an adage true
As human wisdom ever drew!
That this I've practised through my life,
I have a witness in my wife;
For though she'd sometimes snarl and
scold,
I never would a parley hold;
And when she, though but seldom, swore,
I checked the oath, but said no more,
And all returning taunts forbore.
I dressed my spirit from the pages
Of learned Dons and ancient Sages:
But my lean form was never smart
From barber's skill or tailor's art;
So that my figure was a joke
For all the town and country folk.

But this my feelings never grieved,
And I with smiles their smiles received:
I ne'er retorted, like a fool,
Their inoffensive ridicule.

"So that my Dolly's clothes were fine,
She never cared a doit for mine:
So that on every Sabbath-day,
She could appear in trappings gay,
And in a pew her form display,
She'd let me walk about the town,
Till my black coat was almost brown.
But she was, and I can't deny,
The soul of notability.
She struggled hard to save the pelf;
And, though she might except herself,
I do believe, upon my word,
To all things SYNTAX was preferred.

"Bear and forbear, I've thought and said,
Is part of every Parson's trade;
And what he doth to others preach
He should by his example teach.
Whene'er the scoffer trotted by,
I ne'er have turned an angry eye:
Nay, when of Wealth I've been the jeer,
When petty Pride let loose a sneer,
I never failed the joke to join,
And paid them off in classic coin.

"My Rector, fat as fat can be,
With prebend stall, and livings three,

Once told me if I kept my riches
Within the pockets of my breeches,
To make them of materials stout,
Or else the weight would wear them out.
O, with what base, irreverent glee
He chose to mock my poverty!
Yet I did not my cloth disgrace
By squirting spittle in his face;
But answered from St. Paul, in Greek,
And bid him the quotation seek
In Pliny:—When the purse-proud brute
Nodded assent—and then was mute.

"The Oilman there, in that fine house,
Who boasts the escutcheons of his spouse,
Soon after he had left off trade,
Loved some great, noble Lady's maid,
Who by my Lord had been betrayed:
To Hymen's Fane the fair he led,
And gave the claim to half his bed.
She talks of Duchesses by dozens,
As if they were her cater-cousins.
He once said—'Doctor, do you see?
Let's hear what is your pedigree;'—
When I, with reverence due, replied,
'I am not to the great allied;
But yet I've heard my grandame say,
(Though many a year has passed away
Since she is gone where all must go,
Whether they have been high or low,)
That one of our forefathers bore
A place of state in days of yore;

That he was butler or purveyor,
Or trumpeter to some Lord Mayor,
When Carthaginian Hannibal
Dined with his Lordship at Guildhall:
That great man being forced to come,
By order of the Pope of Rome,
To end some quarrel 'tween the houses
That bore the pale and crimson roses.'
The Oilman said, 'It might be so:
And 'twas a monstrous while ago.'

"'Tis thus I give these fools a poke,
And foil their tauntings with a joke;
For that man has no claim to sense,
Whose blood boils at impertinence.
Were I to scourge each fool I meet,
I ne'er must go into the street;
I ne'er my bearded head must pop
Into the chattering barber's shop.

"Bear and forbear—a maxim true
As erring mortals ever knew
But things are changed; new scenes appear
My mind to soothe, my heart to cheer;
The Powers above my fate regard,
And give my patience its reward.
But while I trod Life's rugged road,
While troubles haunted my abode,
With not an omen to portend
That toil would cease, that things would mend,
I did to my allotment bow,
And smoked my pipe as I do now.

"Hail social tube! thou foe to Care!
Companion of my easy chair!
Formed not, with cold and Stoic art,
To harden, but to soothe the heart!
For Bacon, a much wiser man
Than any of the Stoic clan,
Declares thy power to control
Each fretful impulse of the soul;
And Swift has said, (a splendid name,
On the large sphere of mortal fame,)
That he who daily smokes two pipes
The tooth-ache never has—nor gripes.
With these, in silence calm and still,
My Dolly's tones, no longer shrill,
Though meant to speak reproach and
sneer,
Passed in soft cadence to my ear.
Calm Contemplation comes with thee,
And the mild maid,—Philosophy!
Lost in the thoughts which you suggest
To the full counsel of my breast,
My books all slumbering on the shelf,
I thus can commune with myself;
Thus to myself my thoughts repeat;
Thus moralize on what is great,
And, every selfish wish subdued,
Cherish the sense of what is good.

"While I thy grateful breath inhale,
I see the cheering cup of ale;
Benignant juice; Lethean stream!
That aids the fond oblivious dream;

Which fits the freshened mind to bear
The burden of returning care.

"Let Pride's loose sons prolong the night
In Bacchanalian delight;
I envy not their jovial noise,
Their mirth, and mad, intemperate joys.
The luscious wines that Spain can boast,
Or grow on Lusitanian coast,
Ne'er filled my cups:—*Repast divine!
The home brewed beverage is mine.
Thus cheered with hopes of happier days,
My grateful lips declare thy praise.
How oft I've felt in adverse hour,
The comforts of thy soothing power!
Nor will I now forget my friend,
When my foul fortune seems to mend:
Yes, I would smoke as I do now,
Though a proud mitre decked my brow.

"Hail, social tube! thou foe to care!
Companion of my easy chair!
While, as the curling fumes arise,
They seem the ascending sacrifice
That's offered by my gratitude
To the Great Father of the good."

More had he spoke: but, lo! the Dame
With the appointed hazlet came:

———

*————Mea nec Falernæ
Temperant vites, neque Formiani
Pocula colles. Hor. L. i. Od. xx.

When Syntax, having blessed the meat,
Sat down to the luxuriant treat.
"And now," he said, "my dear, 'twill be
As good as Burgundy to me,
If you will tell me what has passed
Since we embraced each other last."
"O," she replied, "my dearest love,
Things in their usual order move.
Pray take a piece of this fine liver:
The Rector is as proud as ever.
I'll help you, dear, to this or that:
Let me supply your lean with fat.—
I thought the Oilman's wife would burst
When in this dress she saw me first:
It was at Church she showed her airs:
My bonnet spoiled the woman's prayers.
Your knife is blunt; here, take the steel:
Cut deep,—the hazlet cannot feel.—
There's Lawyer Graspall got a beating,
As you may well suppose,—for cheating:
Our honest Butcher trounced him well,
As the Attorney's bones can tell.
He ordered home a rump of beef;
And when it came, the hungry thief,
Having shaved off a pound or two,
Returned it for it would not do.
The fraud discovered, words arose,
And they were followed soon by blows:
When, as he well deserved, the sinner
Got a good thrashing for his dinner."

Said Syntax, "If I had a son."
"Pooh!" she replied, "you have not done:
You still, I hope, can pick a bit,
And no excuse will I admit.
'Tis long since we've together been;
Since we've each other's faces seen;
And, surely, I'm not such a fright
To make you lose your appetite."
"But," he continued, "if a boy
Were, my dear Doll, to crown our joy,
I'd sooner, far, the stripling see
The heir of dire Adversity
Than to a dire Attorney bind him,
Where Old Nick is sure to find him."
She added—"Yes, with naked feet
I'd sooner have him pace the street;
But ere you let your choler burst,
Let's have the little urchin first."

The Doctor thought his jolly wife
Ne'er looked so handsome in her life.
Her voice he thought grown wondrous
sweet;
To him a most uncommon treat:
So much in tune, it made him long
To hear it quaver in a song.
"Come, sing, my charmer," Syntax said,
And thus the simpering dame obeyed.

SONG.

"Haste to Dolly! haste away!
This is thine and Hymen's day!

Bid her thy soft bondage wear;
Bid her for Love's rites prepare.
Let the nymphs with many a flower,
Deck the sacred nuptial bower;
Thither lead the lovely fair,
And let Cupid, too, be there.
This is thine and Hymen's day!
Haste to Dolly! haste away!"

Thus passed the time; the morrow came,
And Mrs. Syntax was the same:
But when (for 'twas not done before)
She heard the Doctor's story o'er,
With all the hopes he had in store,
By joy, by vanity subdued,
Her warm embraces she renewed;
While he delighted fondly kissed
Those hands, which, formed into a fist,
Had often warned his eyes and nose
To turn from their tremendous blows.

At length of golden ease possessed,
No angry words, no frowns, molest;
No symptoms of domestic strife
Disturbed their very altered life,
For she out-dressed the Oilman's wife;
And he could now relieve the poor,
Who sought his charitable door.

Though to each virtue often blind,
The world to wealth is ever kind;

For, lo! a certain tell-tale dame,
Ycleped and known as Mistress Fame,
Had told to all the country round
That Syntax for a thousand pound,
Had sold a learned book he wrote:
That now he was a man of note,
By Lords protected! and that one
Would make him tutor to his son:
So that, whenever he went forth,
All paid their homage to his worth;
While it became the fond desire
Of every neighbouring rural 'Squire
To send his hopeful boys to share
The favour of the Doctor's care.

But all these views soon found an end
A packet came, and from a friend;
From 'Squire Worthy, who resides
On Keswick's bold and woody sides.
The wondering Postman made it known,
As he passed on, to all the town;
For such a letter ne'er had been
Within his little circuit seen:
Nay, by the fiat of the Post,
It more than seven shillings cost.
The Doctor stared—while ma'am un-
willing,
Slowly drew forth each lingering shilling.
"Ne'er mind your silver," Syntax said,
"The Postman, Deary, must be paid;
And now these papers I behold,
I see they're worth their weight in gold:

Come, sit you down, and take good heed
To what I'm now about to read."

"Good Reverend Sir,
Our Vicar's dead,
And I have named you in his stead.
I often wished his neck he'd break,
Or tumble drunk into the Lake;
So, you must know the poaching hound
Fulfilled one wish—for he is drowned.
Unfit for preaching or for praying,
His merit lay in cudgel-playing:
And he preferred to saying prayers,
The laying springes for the hares.

"You will perceive I keep my word,
And to this Church you're now preferred:
By every legal act and deed,
To Parson Hairbrain you succeed:
The papers which you now receive,
A right and full possession give.
You, Sir, may make the living clear
Above three hundred pounds a year;
And if you will but condescend
To my son's learning to attend;
If you direct his studious hour,
I'll add some fifty pounds or more:
And soon we hope that you will cheer
The parish with your presence here.
Miss Worthy and her sister join
Their kindest compliments to mine;

And to your prayers I recommend
Your faithful and admiring friend,
JONATHAN WORTHY."

The Dame exclaimed, "My Grecian boy,
I know not how to tell my joy.
This is the height of my desire:—
'Squire Worthy is a worthy 'Squire."

"Ha, ha," said Syntax, "O, the fun!
Why, Dolly, you have made a pun.
But still a pun I do detest,
'Tis such a paltry, humbug jest;
They who've least wit can make them
best.
But you may frisk and pun away;
I'm sure I cannot teach to-day,
So tell the boys to go and play.
Thank Heaven, that, toil and trouble past,
My holidays are come at last!"

At length, the busy school resigned,
They both rejoiced to leave behind
A place which little had to give
Than the hard struggle how to live.
For the long journey to prepare,
Syntax had bought a one-horse chair,
With harness for the grizzle-mare.
Ralph would not from his master part,
But trudged beside the farmer's cart
That bore the Doctor's books and chattels,
With Madam's clothes and fiddle-faddles;

The Cook upon the baggage rode,
And added to the weighty load;
For she, kind maid, was fully bent
To go wherever Ralpho went.
The Doctor walked about to tell
The day when he should say—farewell!
And they who had disdained before
To pass the threshold of his door,
When Syntax gave his farewell treat,
Sought that same door to drink and eat.
The neighbours now, who never yet
Knew his great worth, his loss regret;
While Madam, on whom no good word
Had been, throughout the town, preferred,
Was now a most delightful creature,
Of temper mild,—of winning feature.
The Ringers, who, for many a year,
Refused his natal day to cheer,
Now made the bells, in woeful zeal,
Chime forth the dumb, lamenting peal.
—The time soon came, when, quite light-
hearted,
The Doctor and his spouse departed;
And as they journeyed on their way,
They did not fail to pass a day
At Oxford with his early friend,
The kind and learned Dicky Bend.
Nor did he think it a delay,
The Christian Vicar to repay,
And 'neath his roof a night to stay;
To add, for former kindness shown,
His Dolly's greeting to his own.

At York they formed the pleasant party,
For a whole week, of 'Squire Hearty.

A few days more, and, lo! the Lake
Did on the enraptured vision break:
And, rising 'mid the tufted trees,
Syntax his sacred structure sees,
Whose tower appeared in ancient pride,
With the warm Vicarage by its side.
"At length, dear wife," he said, "we're come
To our appointed, tranquil home."

The courteous people lined the way,
And their rude, untaught homage pay:
The foremost of the assembled crowd,
The fat Exciseman, humbly bowed:
"Welcome," he said, "to SOMMERDEN."
The Clerk stood by, and cried, "Amen!"
Grizzle dashed boldly through the gate,
Where the kind 'Squire and ladies wait,
With kind embrace, with heart and hand,
To cheer them into CUMBERLAND.
The bells rang loud, the boys huzzaed:
The bonfire was in order laid;
The villagers their zeal display,
And ale and crackers close the day.

Syntax, whom all desired to please,
Enjoyed his hours of learned ease;
Nor did he fail to preach and pray,
To brighter worlds to point the way;

While his dear spouse was never seen
To show ill-nature or the spleen;
And faithful Grizzle now no more
Or drew a chaise, or rider bore.

Thus the good Parson, Horse, and Wife,
Led a most comfortable life.

THE END.

www.ingramcontent.com/pod-product-compliance
Lightning Source LLC
LaVergne TN
LVHW020236110826
845151LV00003B/943

* 9 7 8 1 4 2 5 5 3 0 4 9 5 *